Conflict, People & Power

Medieval Britain 1066–1500

MARTYN WHITTOCK

Hodder & Stoughton

A MEMBER OF THE HODDER HEADLINE GROUP

Acknowledgements

The front cover shows the Battle of Agincourt reproduced courtesy of ET Archives, and a portrait of Henry V (1387–1422) (oil on panel) by English School (15th Century) reproduced courtesy of the National Portrait Gallery, UK/ Bridgeman Art Library.

The publishers would like to thank the following individuals, institutions and companies for permission to reproduce copyright illustrations in this book:

Aerofilms Limited p14 (top), 15 (bottom); Ancient Art & Architecture Collection Ltd p52; The Ashmolean, Oxford p7 (left); The Bodleian Library p25, 49 (right); The Bridgeman Art Library p2, 4, 5 (both), 30, 63; The British Library p20, 33, 35, 39 (all), 48, 49 (left), 51 (top); The British Museum p7 (right); King's College Foundation Charter, Cambridge University Library p19; Corbis p14 (bottom); Corpus Christi College, Cambridge p17; English Heritage Photographic Library p15 (top left) (Andrew Tryner), 36 (© Crown Copyright. NMR), 42, 43, 46; e.t. archive, Musee de l'Assistance Publique p50; Hulton Getty p53; A.F. Kersting p 13; Life File/Nigel Shuttleworth p31; The Royal Library, Windsor Castle p9; The Marquis of Salisbury p45; The National Museums & Galleries of Wales p58; The Wellcome Institute Library, London p51 (bottom); Welsh Historic Monuments/T Ball p15 (right).

The publishers would also like to thank the following for permission to reproduce material in this book:

Blackwell Publishers for the extract from *Economic History Review*, Vol L1, No. 2, May 1998 by M Bailey and for the extract from *Peasant Life in the Medieval West* by R Fossier, 1988; Boydel & Brewer Ltd for the extracts from *The Normans and the Norman Conquest* by R Allen Brown, 1985; Cambridge University Press for the extracts from *Medieval Women* by E Power, 1975, and *The Agrarian History of England and Wales 2, 1942-1350* by H E Hallam, 1988; Curtis Brown on behalf of Philip Ziegler for the extracts from *The Black Death* copyright © Philip Ziegler 1982; Extracts from *Anglo-Saxon Chronicle*, edited by GN Garmonsway, 1972,
reprinted by permission of Everyman Publishers PLC; ITPS Ltd for extracts from *The Fourth Estate* by S Shahar, 1983; Macmillan Press Ltd for the extracts from *The Making of Britain: The Middle Ages*, (ed.) L Smith, 1985; The extracts from *The Revolt of Owain Glyndwr* by R R Davies, 1995, have been adapted by permission of Oxford University Press; The extract from *Magna Carta* (Introduction by D Stroud), published 1980, by Paul Cave Publications Ltd; *The Pelican History of England 3: English Society in the Early Middle Ages* by Doris Mary Stenton, Penguin Books, 1951, fourth edition, 1965, copyright © Doris Mary Stenton, 1951, 1952, 1962, 1965, reproduced by permission of Penguin Books Ltd; Pearson Education Ltd for the extract from *King John* by R Turner, 1994, Addison Wesley Longman; Phoenix House for the extract from *Medieval Women* by H Leyser, 1995; Extracts from *Life in a Monastery*, 1998 © Pitkin Unichrome Ltd by Stephen Hebron; Sutton Publishing for extracts from *Military Campaigns of the Wars of the Roses* by P Haigh, 1995 and *New Towns of the Middle Ages* by M Berisford, 1988; Weidenfeld and Nicolson for the extract from *Ireland* by R Kee, 1980.

Comic strip p22 from *Horrible Histories: The Measly Middle Ages*, text © Terry Deary, 1996, Illustrations © Martin Brown 1996, first published by Scholastic Ltd.

Please note that some sources have been adapted to make them more accessible to students.

Every effort has been made to trace and acknowledge ownership of copyright. The publishers will be glad to make suitable arrangements with any copyright holders whom it has not been possible to contact.

The author would like to thank Andrew Deathe of Salisbury and South Wilts Museum, for help regarding the Medieval landscape and route ways around Old Sarum; Bob Mann for help regarding Medieval Totnes; Cathy Houghton at English Heritage, for help finding comparative reconstruction drawings of a Medieval town.

To Richard, Jane, Edward and Harry Butler, in thanks for their friendship.

Orders: please contact Bookpoint Ltd 130 Milton Park, Abingdon, Oxon, OX14 4SB
Telephone: (44) 01235 827720, Fax: (44) 01235 400454. Lines are open from 9.00 - 6.00, Monday to Saturday, with a 24 hour message answering service.
You can also order through our website at www.hodderheadline.co.uk

British Library Cataloguing in Publication Data
A catalogue record for this title is available from The British Library

ISBN 0 340 73045 5

First published 2000
Impression number   10 9 8 7
Year   2005 2004

Copyright © 2000 Martyn Whittock

Typeset by Liz Rowe
Printed in Dubai for Hodder & Stoughton Educational, a division of Hodder Headline, 338 Euston Road, London LW1 3BH

Contents

1 THE NORMAN CONQUEST

THIS CHAPTER ASKS

Why is the year 1066 so important?
Why were there three rivals for the English throne?
Why did Harold lose the battle of Hastings?
How much did the Norman Conquest change England?

NEW WORDS

CONQUEST: to capture or take over something.

OATH: a special promise which should never be broken.

1066 AND ALL THAT...

How many dates of important events in British History do you know? The chances are that one of them is 1066. Many people remember this date even if they do not know any others! It is the date of the Norman **Conquest**. In 1066, Duke William, the ruler of Normandy invaded England. Normandy is in France, but in 1066 it had its own ruler and was separate from the kingdom of France.

William killed the English king, Harold, at the Battle of Hastings. William went on to be crowned King of England on Christmas Day, 1066. He had made himself ruler of Normandy and England. Historians call England before 1066, 'Anglo-Saxon England'. After 1066 they call it 'Norman England'. Kings of England continued to also be rulers of Normandy until the 13th Century.

We call William of Normandy 'William the Conqueror', because he defeated Harold at Hastings. In 1066 many people knew him as 'William the bastard', because his parents were not married.

SOURCE A

◄ A scene from the Norman Bayeux Tapestry, showing King Harold in January 1066. The star in the sky is Halley's comet, which people thought was a sign that big events were coming.

RIVALS FOR THE ENGLISH THRONE

Why did William of Normandy think he should be King of England? Well, in 1066 there were actually three people who thought they should be king!

Each one of these rivals had his own reason for being king. But only one could be king. By the end of 1066 two were dead. Each had died in battle. Only William survived to be the king.

Who should be king?

The last king – Edward – said I should be king just before he died, in January 1066.

I am the most powerful man in England.

The other powerful Anglo-Saxons agreed I should be king.

I became king in January 1066 and was killed at Hastings by William, in October 1066.

Harold Godwinson

Harald Hardrada

The last Viking king of England – Cnut – ruled Denmark and England.

In 1038, Cnut's son promised that the king of Norway should rule Denmark and England after he died.

I invaded England in September 1066. Harold Godwinson killed me at the battle of Stamford Bridge.

William

Edward hated Harold's family. Harold's father murdered Edward's brother

In 1051 Edward promised I should be king.

In 1064 Harold swore an oath to support me.

I invaded England and killed Harold at Hastings. I became king in December 1066.

Q **1.** Carry out a survey of your friends and family. What important dates do they know from British History and why?

2. Design three Spidergrams to show the reasons why each of the three rivals in 1066 thought they should be king of England. Which rival do you think had the strongest claim and why?

Discussion Point

How do we choose our government today? Is it a better way?

Why did Harold lose at Hastings?

SHORT-TERM AND LONG-TERM CAUSES

When historians look at why events happen they often divide them into different kinds of reasons (or 'causes'). Things that happen some time before the event are called 'long-term causes'. Things that happen close to the event are called 'short-term causes'.

In October 1066 William defeated Harold at the Battle of Hastings. But why did he win? What different causes were there? What kinds of evidence will help us find out? Like a detective, historians have to look at all the clues.

NEW WORDS

CHRONICLE: A book listing events in the order in which they happened. It does not explain things the way most history books do.

TIMELINE OF EVENTS BEFORE THE BATTLE OF HASTINGS

- **Friday September 8th.** Harold had kept an army on the south coast in case William invaded. He decided William would not invade and let his army go home.
- **Wednesday September 20th.** Harald Hardrada invades England and defeats an Anglo-Saxon army at Fulford, near York.
- **Monday September 25th.** Harold defeats Harald Hardrada at the Battle of Stamford Bridge, near York. Many are killed on both sides.
- **Wednesday September 27th.** A change in the wind allows William to sail to England with his army across the English Channel.
- **Sunday October 1st.** Harold, still in York, hears that William has landed in Sussex and is destroying villages owned by Harold's family. Harold marches 190 miles back to London.
- **Thursday October 5th.** Harold arrives in London and spends five days getting a new army together.
- **Friday October 13th.** Late at night, after a 60 mile march from London, Harold's army camps north of Hastings, in Sussex. Harold hopes to catch William by surprise but William discovers that Harold is near him.
- **Saturday October 14th.** At dawn, William moves his army to meet Harold. Battle starts at 9am. William defeats Harold.

SOURCE

Harold gathered a great army and came to oppose him [William] at the old apple tree. And William surprised him before his army was ready. But the king still fought against him very bravely, with those men who supported him.

▲ *From the Anglo-Saxon* Chronicle. *This was written shortly after the battle by supporters of Harold.*

SOURCE B

▲*The Bayeux Tapestry, made shortly after the battle to tell the Norman side of the story. It shows Harold's soldiers on foot facing well armed Norman knights.*

SOURCE C

▲ Another picture from the Bayeux Tapestry. It shows part of the battle where Norman knights retreated. Some English soldiers chased them down the hill and were surrounded and killed. After this the Normans pretended to retreat twice. Each time they killed the English soldiers who chased them and this weakened Harold's army.

SOURCE D

A rumour spread that Duke William was dead. But he shouted 'Look at me - I am alive! And with God's help I will win. What madness makes you run away. There is nowhere to escape to. There is only the sea behind us. We have no choice but to win or die'.

▲ Written by the Norman, William of Poitiers. He wrote shortly after the battle and seems to have got his information from Normans who were there.

SOURCE E

Although Harold knew that some of the bravest men in all England had died in the two battles [Fulford and Stamford Bridge] and his army was not yet gathered together, he did not hesitate to meet his enemy. Nine miles from Hastings he fought them before a third of his army had arrived.

▲ The Worcester Chronicle, 1095. The writer used information from the time.

SOURCE G

▲ The Bayeux Tapestry may show Harold wounded in the eye by an arrow. He was later killed by Norman knights. The Normans had many archers. The English had very few.

Harold's body was so badly chopped up that the Normans were not sure it was his. His girlfriend, Edith, was made to check the bits. Only she could tell it was him because she knew his body so well!

SOURCE F

Many soldiers deserted Harold before the battle. The English army spent the night before the battle drinking and singing. The Normans spent the night praying.

▲ Written by an English writer in about 1125.

Q **1.** Look at each of the sources. Say how much you think you can trust each one and why you think this.

2. Why did Harold lose?

■ Explain the long-term reasons (events before the battle).

■ Explain the short-term reasons (events during the battle).

■ End by saying which reason you think is most important and why.

5

Alric's complaint

YOUR MISSION: did the Norman Conquest change the lives of English people for the worse?

The Domesday Book lists who owned land in England in 1086, twenty years after the Norman Conquest. (See chapter 2 for more about the Domesday Book). At Marsh Gibbon, in Buckinghamshire, the Domesday Book records:
'Alric holds land from William FitzAnsculf. He owned it himself before 1066. But now he has to rent it from William. He is miserable and has a heavy heart.'

Imagine Alric has brought a complaint to a modern court. Alric has had his land taken away and given to one of William the Conqueror's Norman friends. Alric is accusing William the Conqueror of completely changing the lives of English people for the worse. You are the jury. Look at each piece of evidence. Look at the evidence against William. Then at the evidence in his favour. Do you agree, or disagree with Alric's complaint?

SOURCE A

He caused castles to be built which were a terrible burden to poor people. A hard man was the king. He took from his people much money in gold and many more hundreds of pounds in silver. This money he took from his people mostly unjustly. He was very greedy. Whoever killed a deer was to be blinded. The rich complained and the poor were sad. But he did not care if everyone hated him.

▲ *From the Anglo-Saxon Chronicle, 1087. This was the year that William the Conqueror died. The person who wrote this thought William should not have been king of England. Alric will have heard that a Norman castle was built near him, in Oxford, in 1071. The Normans who built it put it right on top of the homes of English people.*

SOURCE B

England has become the home of foreigners and has become their property. You might see great churches rise in every village, town and city. They are built in a way not seen before. But I hear many say it would have been better to have kept the old.

▲ *Written by William of Malmesbury, 1125. Marsh Gibbon had no church, but Alric has heard of Norman rebuilding elsewhere.*

The Case Against William the Conqueror.

'He has completely changed the lives of English people for the worse.'

SOURCE C

The great English people who survived the battles of 1066 live poorer or in exile. Normans have taken their land and their power.

▲ *Historian James Campbell in an essay called, 'Where are the Anglo-Saxons?', 1986.*

SOURCE D

Another sign of a total take-over was the disappearance of English used by the government. The new bosses spoke French and wrote Latin.

The Normans had pulled down every Anglo-Saxon cathedral and abbey and most of the churches too, and had rebuilt them on a much bigger scale, in the Norman version of 'modern' **architecture**.

▲ *Written by the historian, W.L.Warren, in a book, The Middle Ages, 1985.*

The Case in Favour of William the Conqueror.

'Much has not changed. What has changed has been for the better!'

SOURCE E

What effect has the Conquest had on the **peasantry**? Not much. In places the freedom of some peasants who used to be independent has been reduced. On the other hand many who were slaves in 1066 have now achieved some freedom.

▲ *James Campbell, in* Where are the Anglo-Saxons?, *1986.*

SOURCE H

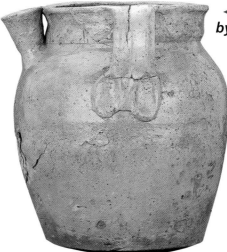

◄ *The kind of pottery used by Alric. It was used around Oxford. These became more popular after the Norman Conquest but were made in the same way as they had been before 1066.*

SOURCE F

King William was a man of great wisdom and power. Though stern to those who opposed him, he was kind to those good men who loved God. We must not forget the peace he kept in the land. Anyone could travel safely across the country with pockets full of gold.

▲ *The Anglo-Saxon Chronicle, 1087.*

SOURCE G

▲ *A silver penny of the kind Alric would have owned. It was made at Oxford by a man named Brihtraed. The same people made the same kinds of money at Oxford before and after the Norman Conquest.*

NEW WORDS

ARCHITECTURE: the way a building is put together.

PEASANTRY: ordinary poor farmers who didn't own the land they worked on.

INVESTIGATION

You are the jury in the court.
From the evidence, you can reach one of three verdicts:

■ William changed things for the worse.
■ William changed things for the better.
■ William changed some things for the worse, some things for the better, some things were not changed much at all.

Whatever you decide, explain why you have reached this decision, mentioning the evidence (**Sources**) you used.

2 AFTER THE CONQUEST – KEEPING CONTROL

THIS CHAPTER ASKS
What problems did William the Conqueror face in controlling England?
How did he deal with these problems?
How and why did castles change and develop during the Middle Ages?

NEW WORDS

ARISTOCRACY: rich landowners.
FEUDAL HOST: the knights sent to fight for William in return for land given to them.
FYRD: local people called to fight for the king in an emergency.
GELDS: tax on the amount of land a person owned.
MERCENARIES: soldiers who fight for anyone who will pay them to fight.
SHIRES: areas of England divided into **hundreds**.

On Christmas day, 1066, William was crowned king of England in Westminster Abbey, London. At his coronation Norman soldiers mistook cheering crowds for rioters and killed many of them. Other Normans, inside the abbey, saw William trembling with fear as he listened to the fighting. He knew he did not really control England.

WILLIAM'S PROBLEMS
Most English people did not support William and would be happy to remove him as ruler.

- There was a threat of invasion from Denmark. After the death of Harald Hardrada, the king of Denmark claimed that he should be king of England. In 1067 and 1069 he sent help to William's English enemies.

- In the north of England many English people had always tried to stay independent of the kings who ruled the south of the country.

- William rewarded his followers with gifts of land, but he needed to keep track of who owned what land.

KEEPING CONTROL – BUILDING CASTLES
When an area was brought under Norman control a castle was built to keep it that way. These castles were called 'motte and baileys'. A wooden tower was built on a mound of earth (the 'motte'). A ditch was dug around the mound. Next to the motte was a flat space where the people in the castle lived. This was the 'bailey'. The bailey was protected by a wooden fence and a ditch. If enemies broke into the bailey, the Normans inside could find shelter on top of the motte. These castles were quick to build. Between 1066 and 1100 the Normans built about 200 castles.

SOURCE A

Though William replaced the Old English **aristocracy** he kept most of the system of government. The **shires** and **hundreds** remained with their courts. William raised **gelds** and so did his sons. He used the system of Anglo-Saxon military service, the **fyrd**, to add to his **mercenaries** and his **feudal host**.

▲ *Historian, James Campbell, in The Anglo-Saxons, 1982. This well organised government helped William keep control.*

KEEPING CONTROL – DEFEATING REBELS

In 1068 William returned to England from Normandy because there had been rebellions against his rule. At Exeter William was not amused when an Englishman bared his bottom over the walls! The Normans defeated the rebels.

In 1068 there was a rebellion in the north. William marched to York, crushed the rebellion and built a castle there. The next year there was a more serious rebellion in the north. Robert, the Norman Earl of Northumbria, and his knights were massacred at Durham, other Normans were killed at York. William defeated the rebels but was so worried he sent his wife, Matilda, back to Normandy for safety. Later in 1069, a Danish fleet helped more English rebels, who killed almost all the Normans in York.

William marched north again. That winter the Norman army destroyed all the farms in Yorkshire, Cheshire, Shropshire, Staffordshire and Derbyshire. Thousands of English people starved to death. New castles were built to keep control of these areas. By the spring of 1070 William was in control. Although there were other rebellions, none of them were as serious as these.

Q

1. Look at the problems William faced in controlling England. For each of his 'problems', explain how well he solved them?

2. Look at **Source A**. How might a historian use this to show that it was not just William's skills and brutality that helped him control England?

3. From all you have seen explain how far you think William was really in control of England by 1070.

SOURCE B

▲ *A modern artist's reconstruction of the first motte and bailey castle at Windsor. It had two baileys.*

KEEPING CONTROL – THE DOMESDAY BOOK

William the Conqueror spent a lot of money fighting wars. In 1071 he crushed a rebellion against him by an army of Danes and Englishmen in East Anglia. One of the rebels, Hereward the Wake, later became famous in legends for holding out against the Normans in the marshes at Ely. He eventually surrendered and was pardoned. In 1075 three of William's **earls** got drunk at a wedding and plotted a rebellion, which was crushed by the king.

In 1085 the king of Denmark planned a great invasion of England. In the end he never sailed, but the danger forced William to pay for a huge army, which he brought from Normandy to England. Then there were wars against the new king of France. Who was going to pay for all this?

THE KING'S GREAT SURVEY

At Christmas 1085, in Gloucester, William put together a plan to find out exactly who owned what land in England. This would make it easier to tax them and control the country. During the first six months of 1086 William's men went out across England. They visited every shire in England. They made a record of:

- Who owned land in 1066 and now (1086).
- What the land was like, how many ploughs could work on it, what kinds of people lived there.
- How much the land was worth in 1066 and 1086.

The great survey was finished in the summer of 1086. It was then put together in a great collection, which came to be called the 'Domesday Book'. This means 'judgement day', as it was thought the king had found out everything there was to know about people. This reminded people of the Christian belief in the Day of Judgement, when God will examine what everyone has done with their lives.

WHAT THE DOMESDAY BOOK CAN TELL US

Domesday Book is like a window to help us look back in time. It tells us who owned land, what different kinds of people lived in the country, what the land was like and how farming was organised. It shows what land was worth.

As importantly, it shows how powerful and well organised William's government was. He made sure England was more under the control of the king than it had ever been before. But he could not have carried out his great survey without using the well organised Anglo-Saxon government of the local areas. Domesday Book shows how William took over the English way of running the country and made it even better organised. Later kings would take this further and make themselves even more wealthy and powerful.

NEW WORDS

EARLS: rich and powerful landowners who were responsible for running large areas of the country.
HIDE: an area of land big enough to supply food for a whole family. (In the north of England and in the east Midlands these were called **CARUCATES**.)

SOURCE A

He [William] sent his men all over England into every shire. He had them find out how many hundred **hides** there were in each shire, or what land and cattle the king had in the country or what taxes he ought to have in a year. Also he had a record made of how much land his archbishops had, and his bishops and his abbots and earls and how much money it was worth. There was no single hide nor a yard of land, nor indeed (it is a shame to tell it but he was not ashamed to do it) one ox, one cow, or pig which was left out and not put down in his record.

▲ *Written in the Anglo-Saxon Chronicle for the year 1086. The writer of the Chronicle thought William was wrong to carry out the great survey.*

Here is a part of the Domesday Book in modern English. It is about land at a place called 'Tateshalla', in the West Riding of Yorkshire. Today this is an area of the modern town of Pontefract, called Tanshelf.

Domesday Book contains 2 million words, mentions 13,418 places, is made from the skins of as many as one thousand sheep and was written by only one man!

1 *This shows how much ploughing could be done there. All the money from this land went to the lord.*

2 *This shows it had belonged to King Edward in 1066 but King William has given it to one of his Norman supporters.*

3 *These are townspeople.*

4 *These are poor farmers, who own a cottage but no land.*

In Tateshalla there are 16 **carucates** of land which do not pay tax, where 9 ploughs could work. **1** The king owned this *manor*. Now Ilbert has 4 ploughs there **2** and 60 small *burgesses* **3**, 16 cottagers **4**, 16 villagers **5**, and 8 smallholders **6** who have 18 ploughs. A church is there and a priest. There is a place for fishing, 3 mills worth 42 shillings, 3 acres of meadow and woodland pasture. The value before 1066 was £20, now £15. **7**. Within the manor there is land for the poor **8**.

5 *These are better off farmers.*

6 *These own more land than a cottager but less than a villager.*

7 *This shows what it used to be worth and what it was worth in 1086.*

8 *Domesday Book sometimes has other interesting information too. This shows that money from some land was spent on poor people.*

Q

1. Look at **Source A**. The writer of this was an English person living at Peterborough. Why might he have been so against King William carrying out his great survey?

2. Look at the kinds of things King William's men wanted to find out about each landowner's land. What answers would they have found to these questions when they examined Ilbert's land at Tateshalla?

3. Write a brief report on the Domesday Book. In it explain what problems William faced; why and how he carried out the great survey; what kinds of things it would tell him. Conclude by saying how it helped to solve his problems.

How and why did castles change?

1 *Fire destroyed wooden walls and towers.*

2 *Mines broke down corners of square towers.*

3 *By the 1140s catapults threw stones at walls and 'battering rams' smashed walls.*

4 *By 1270 new ideas were brought from the Middle East: castles with rings of walls.*

5 *After 1450 cannons began to be used.*

CHANGING CASTLES

Between 1066 and 1500 over 1,500 castles were built in England and Wales. Over this time the way they were built changed a great deal. These changes happened for a number of reasons, and some of these are shown in the cartoons on this page. Most of the reasons castles changed were because attackers found new ways of breaking into them. Castle defences needed to change to keep these attackers out.

People attacking castles looked for a castle's weak points. King Richard I built a mighty castle in France called Chateau Gaillard. But it was captured in 1203 when an attacker crawled up the toilet pipe!

FROM WOOD TO STONE

The first 'motte and bailey' castles were made from wood and could easily catch fire. Before the year 1100 castle builders experimented with a new idea. This was a square, stone tower built in the 'bailey' and called a 'keep'. One of the earliest was built by William the Conqueror, in London, by 1087. It became known as the 'White Tower' after it was whitewashed in 1240 and is in the middle of the Tower of London. Other great square keeps were built at Chepstow, Colchester and later at Rochester. The last great square keep was built at Dover in 1189.

Between 1100 and 1150 many wooden towers on mottes were replaced by stone towers called 'shell keeps'. But they were often too heavy for the earth motte.

PROBLEMS WITH SQUARE KEEPS

The square keeps could be captured if attackers broke into one of the square corners. Sometimes they dug a tunnel, called a 'mine', under the corner. Then they set fire to the posts holding up the tunnel and it collapsed, bringing down the corner of the square keep! King John's soldiers did this to Rochester castle in 1215. They used the fat from 40 pigs to set fire to the posts. John said the pigs should be ones not tasty enough for use as bacon!

ROUND TOWERS AND CURTAIN WALLS

Round towers do not have corners! They are harder to break into than towers that do. The first round keep was built at New Buckingham, in Norfolk, in 1146. The idea caught on and between 1180 and 1250 many were built.

From about 1200 more stone walls began to be built around castle baileys. These 'curtain walls' were harder for battering rams and other machines to break into.

Wooden platforms, called 'hourdings', were usually built jutting out from the walls. Through gaps in the floors of these, defenders could fire arrows and drop stones, hot water and **quick lime** on the heads of attackers. The hourdings were later replaced by stone 'parapets' which had gaps in them called 'machicolations'.

CONCENTRIC CASTLES

Crusaders returning from the Middle East brought back the idea of 'concentric castles'. These were defended by rings of walls. When Edward I conquered Wales he built concentric castles between 1272 and 1307, such as that at Beaumaris, Anglesea.

DEFENDING THE WAY IN

Castle gateways had to be strong. By 1300 many round, or 'D-shaped', towers were being built to defend gates. Some stood out from the walls and were called 'barbicans'. The Barbican Centre in London is named after one of the gates of London.

THE COMING OF CANNONS

In the fifteenth century, cannons made it hard to defend castles. Cannon balls could smash walls. Also, there was less fighting in England. Rich people began building undefended country houses not castles.

A CHAIN OF CHANGES...

On this page and on the next two pages are pictures of different castles. They date from different times in the Middle Ages, but they are not put in chronological order. This means they do not appear in the order they were built in over time. They are out of order. Look carefully at them, then attempt the tasks.

NEW WORDS

CRUSADES: wars fought between Christians and Muslims in the Middle East.

QUICK LIME: a terrible liquid that burns a person's body.

SOURCE **A**

▲ *Barbican at Lewes castle, Sussex.*

THINKING IT THROUGH

▲ *Framlingham Castle, Suffolk.*

▲ *Keep of Rochester Castle, Kent.*

SOURCE D

⋀ *Wingfield Manor, Derbyshire. It is a large, undefended, country house.*

SOURCE E

⋀ *Caerphilly Castle, Gwent, Wales.*

SOURCE F

The very first castle to have its wall broken down by a cannon was Bamburgh Castle, Northumberland, in 1464.

◄ *Shell keep at Restormel Castle, Cornwall.*

Q Look at all the evidence about castles then answer this question:

How and why did castles change during the Middle Ages?

- First put each castle in the order in which you think they were built.
- As you do this, explain how each castle was different to the one before.

- Explain why each change took place. What caused it to happen? What problem(s) did it try to solve?
- Write a conclusion in which you say how much castles had changed by the end of the Middle Ages. Think about what changed and what stayed the same.

3 THE CHANGING POWER OF THE KING

THIS CHAPTER ASKS

How and why did kings become more powerful?
What problems did some kings face?
Why did parliament become so important?
How bad was 'bad King John'?
Did Magna Carta really protect English freedom?

Henry II, 1154–89.
Clever soldier, built many
castles. Government well run.

John, 1199–1216.
Short of money, lost wars in
France, fell out with Church
and barons.

Edward I, 1272–1307.
Clever soldier, punished rebels,
built castles. Conquered Wales
and invaded Scotland.

Henry VI, 1422–61, 1470–71.
Defeated by French, mentally
ill, beaten by rivals twice in
Wars of the Roses. Murdered.

▲ *Some strong and weak kings.*

HOW DANGEROUS WAS IT TO BE A KING?

The title of this BIG PICTURE sounds rather sexist. After all, what about the queens? Well, with the exception of the Empress Matilda in the Twelfth Century, every ruler in the Middle Ages was a man. And even Matilda had to fight a **civil war**, because a man – her cousin Stephen – had made himself king before she could be crowned!

Between 1066 and 1500 there were 18 English kings. Of these four were overthrown and murdered. Another one, William II, was killed in a hunting accident in the New Forest which might not really have been an 'accident'. Kings had power and wealth and sometimes other people wanted to take it from them. But most kings did not die this way. Most ruled the land and died in their beds. In fact, by the end of the Middle Ages most kings were more powerful than those at the beginning.

IN WHAT WAYS WERE KINGS STRONGER?

Kings improved the way they collected **taxes**. Around 1110 an organisation called the Exchequer was set up by Roger, Bishop of Salisbury, a trusted friend of King Henry I. Henry liked him because his church services were short. The Exchequer checked all the money that should be paid to the king and kept records of who had paid. This made the king wealthier. More money helped kings to build castles and fight wars. Henry II spent £21,000 on castles. Today this would be worth about £33 billion. This helped kings defeat rivals and rebels and stay in power.

Royal law became better organised. Judges travelled and tried people accused of crimes at county courts called assizes. Records were kept of cases and sentences. Other courts were set up in London to decide on disagreements about land. This meant kings were more in control. And money paid in fines went to the king.

In 1199 King John began keeping a record of all his official letters. This grew into an organisation called the Chancellory. This made it easier to know what was going on in the country and to check decisions kings had made.

WHAT THINGS HELPED INCREASE THE POWER OF KINGS?

Changes in the way the Christian Church was run improved the education of priests. The Church encouraged the setting up of universities such as Oxford and Cambridge. Better educated people were given jobs by the king and helped improve the way the government was run.

When kings respected the Church, it supported them and said it was a sin to rebel because God had given the king his power. This did not always work. Henry II fell out with his friend Thomas Becket, when Thomas became Archbishop of Canterbury. Henry wanted to have more control of the church and, in 1170, Thomas was murdered. But trouble like this did not happen very often.

Success in war helped a king too. He could reward his followers with land and property taken from a defeated enemy. Even if some of the king's **barons** opposed him it was hard to defeat a king who was a skillful soldier.

NEW WORDS

BARONS: the most powerful landowners.
CIVIL WAR: when people from the same country fight each other.
TAXES: money paid to the government.

At Christmas, 1124 the men who made coins for Henry I were accused of stealing silver that should have gone into the coins sent to his army fighting in France. They all had their private parts and right hands cut off.

SOURCE B

Bishops crown him. The Church supports him.

The 'orb' shows he has authority over all his people.

The 'sceptre' shows he has power to carry out justice.

The barons support him.

▲ *Picture of King Edward III at his coronation in 1327. It shows what the artist thought made a king 'strong'.*

Q

1. Make a Spidergram to show ways in which kings became more powerful.

2. Colour code it to show which ways were *religious* (to do with God and the Church), **economic** (to do with money), *political* (to do with how the government worked).

3. Look at **Source A**. Choose two 'strong kings' and explain why they were strong. Then do the same for two 'weak kings'.

4. Does **Source B** show *all* the things that made a king strong?

5. Using all the evidence, explain how and why Medieval kings became more powerful.

Why did Parliament become important?

Today the laws in this country are made by a group of people called Parliament.

THINKING IT THROUGH

WHEN DID PARLIAMENT START?

The word 'parliament' comes from the French word 'parler' meaning 'to talk'. As far back as Anglo-Saxon times the king met with his powerful advisors to help him run the country. The people who came to these meetings were the most powerful landowners. After 1066 William I and the Norman kings met with their barons three times a year. In time these meetings came to be called the 'Great Council'. This was the start of the House of Lords.

In 1258 the English barons had a disagreement with their king, Henry III. They thought he was not running the country properly. They made him discuss the running of the country with the barons. This became known as the 'Parliament'. Really it was just another name for the old Great Council.

SIMON DE MONTFORT AND THE COMMONS.

In 1264 another baron – Simon de Montfort – led a revolt against Henry III. Simon wanted to get more support for his revolt. To do this he invited **commoners** to come to Parliament as well as the barons. Every county sent two **knights** and every important town sent two townspeople. This was the start of the House of Commons. The elections took place at shire (county) and town courts and only the better off people were allowed to vote.

Simon was defeated and killed in 1265. The man who killed him became Edward I. He carried on with Simon's new type of parliament because it was a useful way of getting support for the king and his plans.

WHY PARLIAMENT BECAME POWERFUL.

Kings in the Middle Ages were often short of money. This became more serious after 1290, as kings needed money to fight in Wales, Scotland and France. Between 1200 and 1290 kings had only collected nine great taxes. The next nine taxes were collected in only twenty years. Parliament agreed to pay these taxes.

Until 1356 all the business of Parliament was carried out in French. It changed to English because it did not seem right to use French, as England was fighting the 'Hundred Years War' with France.

NEW WORDS

COMMONERS: people who were not royal, or great landowners.
KNIGHTS: smaller landowners who were given land in return for fighting for their lord. They were often important people in their local community.
SENILE: when an old person is unable to think and understand properly.
SPEAKER: the person who took the demands of parliament to the king.

SOURCE A

What are these worthless knights trying to do? Do they think that they are the kings and princes of this land? Or where have they got their pride and arrogance from?

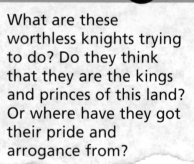 *Spoken by John of Gaunt in 1376, when Parliament refused to agree to new taxes. He was the brother of Edward III. This report of his words was written by Thomas Walsingham who disliked John of Gaunt and thought it right to limit the power of a king if he was behaving badly.*

TROUBLE WITH PARLIAMENT.

As Parliament became more powerful there was sometimes conflict between it and the king. Parliaments tried to make kings spend money wisely. They tried this particularly if the king was weak in some way. For example, this happened in 1376 when Edward III was **senile** and his son, the Black Prince, was dying. In this year the House of Commons elected its first **speaker** to explain why the Commons were so unhappy with the royal government. Kings did not like this because it reduced their power. But they could not get rid of Parliament because they needed the taxes!

SOURCE **B**

The king has asked from the Church and the Commons taxes on wool and other goods. In my opinion it is too much to give him, for the Commons are so weakened by the many taxes which have been paid up to now that they cannot afford such a charge. All the money that we have given for the war has been lost because it has been badly spent.

▲ *Spoken by Peter de la Mare to Parliament in 1376. Peter was the first Speaker of Parliament. He believed that the king, Edward III, was not spending tax money properly.*

SOURCE **C**

◄ *The king and Parliament, fifteenth century. At the top right, God gives power to the king. He shares it with the Lords (below him, on the left) and then with the Commons (below the Lords).*

Q

1. Look at **Sources A** and **B**. What different opinions did these speakers have about the power of Parliament? Look at the information about each Speaker. How might their backgrounds have caused them to think as they did?

2. Look at the information about the writer of **Source A**. How might this affect how reliable this source is?

3. Make a timeline of the events between 1200 and 1376 mentioned in this THINKING IT THROUGH. Mark on it any 'turning points'. These are events which were so important they changed history. Then explain why you chose these.

4. From what you have learned, explain how and why Parliament changed and became more powerful after 1250.

'Bad King John'?

YOUR MISSION: can we trust the evidence that says King John was a bad king?

NEW WORDS

EXCOMMUNICATED: cut off from the Christian Church and from God.
INTERDICT: stopping Church services in a place.
POPE: head of the Christian Catholic Church.
PRIMARY SOURCE: evidence from the time studied.
SECONDARY SOURCE: evidence from later historians.

SOURCE A

▲ John caring for his dogs. Drawn after John died.

SOURCE B

The servant of a sheriff in Wales brought a robber to the royal court who had attacked and killed a priest. 'Let him go', John said, 'He has killed one of my enemies'.

▲ Written by Roger of Wendover. He was a monk at St Alban's Abbey and died in 1236. Like many monks he disliked John because John had fallen out with the pope. He lived at the time of John but is often unreliable.

King John timeline

1199 John becomes king. Short of money, as a lot had been spent by his father, Henry II, and brother, Richard I.

1203 John's rival, Arthur, Duke of Brittany is murdered. Most people agree that John ordered the murder.

1203–4 Defeated in war, John loses his French lands in Normandy, Anjou and much of Poitou

1207 John refused to accept the man the **pope** chose to be Archbishop of Canterbury.

1208 Pope punishes John by putting England under an **Interdict**. No Church services.

1209 John **excommunicated** by the pope. John seizes Church lands and money.

1209 John forced king of Scotland to give up his claim to rule parts of northern England.

1210 John drove rebel barons out of Ireland and defeated Irish princes.

1211 John invaded Wales, partly defeated Welsh.

1213 John gives in to pope and says pope is ruler of England and Ireland.

1214 John tries to recapture lost land in France but is defeated at battle of Bouvines. Short of money, John tries new ways to force it from barons.

1215 English barons rebel against John. They force him to sign an agreement called Magna Carta. This limits his power and protects the rights and freedom of the barons.

1216 More rebellions by barons, who asked the son of the king of France to invade England. John dies.

SOURCE C

There is no one in Ireland, Scotland and Wales who does not obey the commands of the King of England.

▲ *From the Barnwell Chronicle. This was written by a monk between 1210-16. He recorded evidence fairly about John.*

SOURCE D

When he was drunk and possessed by the devil, he killed him with his own hands. He tied a stone round his body and threw it into the River Seine.

▲ *How John killed Arthur, his nephew, according to the monk writing the Margam Chronicle. He lived at the time of John and claimed he heard this from one of John's powerful friends, William de Broase. This friend later became an enemy of John.*

SOURCE E

John was a tyrant, a destroyer, who crushed his own people. He lost the duchy of Normandy and many other territories. He hated his wife and she hated him.

▲ *Written by Matthew Paris. He was a monk at St Alban's Abbey between 1217 and 1259 when he died. Most of what he wrote about John he took from the writing of Roger of Wendover.*

SOURCE F

While John's reign was a failure, he had some successes and even came close to regaining Normandy and defeating the rebel barons. John's efforts in the British Isles made the English kings stronger.

▲ *Historian, Ralph Turner in* King John, *1994.*

SOURCE G

Rumours that the king himself was responsible for the murder of his nephew created an atmosphere of fear. But he was also a generous, able and lavish king.

▲ *Historian, Doris Stenton in* English Society in the Early Middle Ages, *1965.*

INVESTIGATION

You are the investigator!
Does the evidence make you think that John was a 'bad' king? To do this you will need to:

■ Use the BIG PICTURE to explain what made a king 'weak', or 'strong' in the Middle Ages. Then explain that many people thought a 'weak' king was also a 'bad' one.

■ Explain what picture you get of John from the **Primary Sources (Sources A,B,C,D,E)**. Do they agree, or disagree with each other? From what you know about these writers say which you think is reliable and why.

■ Explain what picture you get of John from the **Secondary Sources (Sources F,G)** Do they agree or disagree with each other? Which of the Primary Sources might they have used to get their ideas? Does this affect how reliable you think they are?

■ In your opinion how 'bad' a king was King John? Decide by looking at all the evidence and the 'good' and 'bad' things about his rule.

Did Magna Carta protect freedom?

YOUR MISSION: to explore how far Magna Carta really protected the freedom of ordinary English people.

THE 'GREAT CHARTER'.

In the early summer of 1215 a group of barons rose in revolt against King John. They felt John was ruling badly. His wars were costing a lot of money. To get hold of more money he was doing cruel and unfair things. He charged the barons huge amounts of money to take over their family's land when their father died. For example in 1213 John de Lacey had to pay £4,666 to **inherit** his father's land. Most barons thought it should cost only £100.

John imprisoned those who could not pay him the money they owed him. William de Broase owed John over £3000. He was forced to leave the country, and his wife and son were thrown into prison with only a lump of uncooked bacon to eat. John let them starve to death. When their bodies were finally removed it was found that the son had started to eat his dead mother before he too finally died.

In June 1215 the king met the barons at Runnymede, in Surrey. They forced him to sign a document called 'The Articles of the Barons'. From 1217 this became known as Magna Carta ('Great **Charter**' in Latin). It listed the rights and freedoms that free men should have and forced the king to agree to protect these freedoms. But did Magna Carta really protect the freedom of ordinary English people?

SOURCE B

To commemorate Magna Carta, symbol of freedom under the law.

▲ *The words on a monument set up at Runnymede, where King John signed Magna Carta.*

SOURCE C

By mid July John had written to the pope asking him to cancel the charter. By the autumn the rebels had realised that the king had no intention of keeping his promises. They sent a request for help to France. They offered the throne to Prince Louis and he accepted. Denounced by the king, discarded by the rebels, Magna Carta was surely dead.

▲ *Historian, John Gillingham in* The Making of Britain: The Middle Ages, *1985.*

SOURCE A

WHAT'S THIS THEN? — IT'S A MAGNA CARTA, ISN'T IT

WHAT'S THAT MEAN? — ER...WELL, MAGNA'S LIKE MAGNET. AND A MAGNET HAS POWER

AND CARTA? — CARTA'S LIKE-LIKE CARTERS. ORDINARY PEOPLE

SO MAGNA CARTA MEANS... POWER TO THE PEOPLE!

▲ *A joke from* Horrible Histories: The Measly Middle Ages, *by Terry Deary, 1988.*

SOURCE D

All freemen are granted the freedoms listed below.
  The English Church shall be free and shall have all her rights and freedoms untouched.
  An heir shall inherit on payment of the usual payment.
  No widow will be forced to remarry.
  No tax shall be forced on the kingdom without the common agreement of the kingdom.
  No freeman shall be imprisoned without trial.
  To no one will we sell, or refuse, or delay justice.
  The barons shall choose any 25 barons they wish so that if we or our servants break this agreement they shall seize our castles, lands and property.

▲ *Some of the main points of the 63 articles in Magna Carta. But remember: in 1215 most people in England were not free and Magna Carta promised them nothing; most of the rights protected in Magna Carta were those of rich landowners. The barons set up a group to make sure the country was run in the way the barons liked.*

INVESTIGATION

You are the investigator!
You are a member of the group Amnesty International which tries to protect people's rights and freedoms. You are looking at how much Magna Carta really protected the freedom of ordinary English people. To do this you need to:

■ Explain what it tried to do.
■ Decide who it was meant to protect.
■ Decide how successful it was at the time and later (and why).

SOURCE E

Many of the parts of Magna Carta fell into disuse over time. On the other hand, as the originally small group of 'free men' grew to include every citizen, the parts that remained became relevant to everyone. When in the seventeenth century Englishmen were again seeking to control the king they turned to Magna Carta as a basic statement that the law was more powerful than the king. In 1776 and more than three thousand miles away another group of rebels included the ideas of Magna Carta and even used similar words in their Declaration of Independence which led to the Constitution of the United States of America.

▲ *Daphne Stroud in* Magna Carta, 1980. *The 'Constitution of the USA' is the set of rules which explains how the USA should be run. It was written when the Americans broke away from being ruled by Britain in the eighteenth century.*

King John eventually died in 1216 after a meal in which he ate too many peaches and drank too much new cider.

4 THE IMPACT OF CHRISTIANITY

THIS CHAPTER ASKS
How big an impact did Christian beliefs have on people's lives?
Did religious ideas change during the Middle Ages?
What was it like to be a nun?

NEW WORDS

ABBEY/MONASTERY: place where monks and nuns worship God, away from the world.
PRIEST: a person who led Church services and looked after the local church.
SAINT: a dead, holy person who was thought to help answer prayers.
SIN: wrong doing deserving punishment in Hell. God would judge sinners.

MEMBERS OF CHRISTENDOM

Almost everybody living in Britain in the Middle Ages would have described themselves as members of the Christian Church. The exception would have been the fairly small community of Jewish people. But in 1290 King Edward I forced them to leave England, taking only what they could carry with them. For years they had been badly treated. Jews were distrusted because they were not Christians and were often attacked and sometimes killed. They were forced to give loans and gifts of money to the king and only allowed to do the unpopular work of money lenders. This was unpopular with many people because they had to pay back to the Jews more money than they had borrowed from them.

All the Christian people were members of one Christian group – the Catholic Church – whose leader, called the pope, lived in Rome. Most people across Europe were also members of the Catholic Church. Along with other Christians in the Middle East they made up *Christendom*, the name for the great community of all Christians.

THE CHURCH OF GOD

The Medieval Church was powerful, rich and well organised. It united rich and poor, old and young. It had its own language, Latin, which had once been the language of the Roman Empire. This became the language used in Church services and was the language used by all educated people in Europe. The Church ran all education and the first universities, such as Oxford and Cambridge, were originally run by the Church. It even had its own laws (called Canon Law) and courts which looked after the running of the Church and punished people who disobeyed the leaders of the Church.

Everyone went to church and there were many services in the week and a great many churches. In York there was one church for every 243 inhabitants and this was not unusual. The people who ran the services in these churches were **priests**.

SOURCE A

We curse them sleeping, or walking. That the pains of Hell shall be their drink with Judas who betrayed our Lord Jesus Christ and they shall be taken out of the Book of Life until they change their ways.

▲ *From a Medieval service of 'Excommunication'. This was thought to cut a person off from the Church and from God. It was done to people who had rebelled against the Church.*

In 1381 there were over 29,000 clergy in England. This was one for every fifty people in the country! The same proportion today would come to over one million.

Medieval Christians believed their priests had the power to act for God to forgive, or punish their **sins**. Priests were not supposed to marry, although some lived with women as if they were their wives. Altogether, there was a huge group of people who helped run the church and who were known as the 'clergy', or 'clerks'. Some, like priests and also monks and nuns in **monasteries**, were not allowed to marry. Others who were called 'clerks in minor orders' included those who cared for church buildings, helped run the Church organisation and even every university student. These 'clerks in minor orders' could marry and could work outside the Church.

In the fourteenth century about a quarter of all the land in England was owned by the Church. Rich people gave land to the Church to please God. The money from this land helped pay for the running of the Church. It was said that if the Abbot of Glastonbury **Abbey** married the Abbess of Shaftesbury Abbey, then their child would be richer than the king of England! Of course, they were not really allowed to marry. This was a Medieval joke.

The Christian message of the Church gave people in the Middle Ages - as today – hope in life after death, a belief that life had a purpose, advice on living a good and loving life and the comfort of believing that God loved and would help them. Medieval Christians also believed that they could pray to the Virgin Mary and to **saints** to help them too.

SOURCE B

▲ A painting from 1450. It shows sinners being punished in Hell.

SOURCE C

Christ's rules and his apostles twelve, He taught – but first he followed it himself.

▲ From the fourteenth century poem, the Canterbury Tales, by Geoffrey Chaucer. Here he describes a poor priest who spends his life lovingly serving his people.

Q

1. Look carefully at **Sources A** and **B**. How does this evidence help explain why the Church was so powerful in the Middle Ages.

2 'The Church was not only powerful because people were afraid of going to Hell. It was also powerful because it helped them live their lives.' Using **Source C** and any other information you can find, explain why this statement is true.

Discussion Point
What is the most important belief you have? Why is this belief so important to you?

CONFLICT AND COMPLICATIONS.

In the 1080s, King William II told the **Archbishop** of Canterbury to 'clear off'. Knights of Henry II murdered another Archbishop of Canterbury in 1170. In the thirteenth century, King John is reported to have said to a deer he had just killed during a hunt, *'I envy you, lucky animal, at least you don't have to go to Church services'*. Although English kings gave land and wealth to the Church they wanted to be in control of it. In 1345, Pope Clement VI said, *'If the king of England were to ask for his donkey to be made a **bishop**, we must not disagree with him'*.

So, not everybody got on well with the Christian Church, or treated it with respect. Many ordinary people in the countryside were not happy having to give a 'tithe' (a tenth) of all they produced to the church. In the fifteenth century there are many examples of villagers **castrating** local priests they thought had forced women to have sex with them.

Many local priests were poor, badly educated and could hardly read the Latin in church services. Few of them owned a Bible, as it cost ten years' wages for a poor priest.

Think again...

But these problems are misleading. When King William II was very ill, in 1093, he prayed to God, asking God to forgive him all his sins. He gave back land he had stolen from the Church. Henry II was so sorry about what his knights had done that he knelt, barefoot, in Canterbury Cathedral, while monks whipped him. In 1210, King John was the first English ruler to give clothes and money to poor people on **Maundy Thursday**, after he had washed their feet. He was copying something Jesus had done the night before he was crucified. Even when Medieval kings had a row with the Church they still believed in Christianity. And none of them wanted to die without having made up with the Church.

Medieval kings could not have run the country without the help of educated priests. In the fourteenth century half of all the bishops in the country also had jobs running the government as well. This sometimes meant that people became bishops more because the king liked them than because they lived good and holy lives. But it still shows that the king relied on the Church.

And what about those attacks on priests? Well, even this shows that people expected something special from the Church. They thought it was important. They were angry when they were let down by people they felt they should be able to respect and trust.

NEW WORDS

ARCHBISHOP: an important Church leader. The Archbishop of Canterbury was head of the Church in England.

BISHOPS: important Church leaders, under an archbishop.

CASTRATE: to cut off a man's private parts.

MAUNDY THURSDAY: the Thursday before Easter, when Christians celebrate Jesus sharing the Last Supper with his followers.

Any Medieval person who could translate the first verse of Psalm 51, in the Bible, into Latin could claim 'benefit of clergy'. This meant they could not be hanged even if they had murdered someone. It became known as the 'neck verse'.

The Impact of Christianity in the Middle Ages

(The Church gives us work.)

(We pay priests to pray for merchants.)

(The Church gives us celebrations to remind us of God's love.)

(God gives power to the king, the king gives power to me.)

(I was baptised and made a member of the Christian Church.)

(When I die, I will go to heaven.)

(I stand between people and God. I hear about their sins. I forgive them.)

(The Church gives me education.)

Q

1. Why was verse 1 of Psalm 51 called the 'neck verse'?

Look up this verse in the Bible. Why do you think this particular verse was chosen? Look at what it is about.

2. Explain how the evidence on the opposite page shows:

  a. The Church was not always popular.

  b. The Church always remained powerful, despite this.

3. From the clues in this BIG PICTURE, write about 'the impact of the Christian Church on people's lives'. Mention:

- The comfort and hope it gave them.
- How it helped organise their lives.
- The work it provided.
- Things people might sometimes have not liked.

So, how important was the Church in the Middle Ages?

A changing Church?

THE SAME BUT NOT QUITE?

At the end of the fifteenth century, a visitor to England from Venice wrote about how many churches he saw and how English people loved Church services and believed deeply in God. The Church seemed as powerful as ever. But changes were happening.

FORCES FOR CHANGE

Between 1350 and 1500 problems in farming and the Black Death caused problems in the **economy**. People had less money to give to the Church. Many people were unhappy with how the Church was run and also disliked giving money to a foreign pope in Italy and having English monasteries controlled by monks in foreign countries.

For years keen people, who wanted to live holy lives, had become monks and nuns. At first the biggest group were black-robed and called *Benedictines*. In 1131 a new group - white-robed *Cistercians* - set up their first monastery in a wild Yorkshire valley, at Rievaulx. They said Benedictines had become too rich and had stopped living strict enough lives. But by 1200 the Cistercians, with their sheep farms, had become rich too. In the 1220s a new group of monks arrived – *Friars*. Started by the Italian, St Francis, they wandered the country preaching about Jesus and begging for food. In 1215 Pope Innocent III decided there should be no new groups of monks and nuns. But soon the Friars grew rich; people felt they too had stopped living holy lives.

A NEW WAY FORWARD?

When people spent money on churches it began to go to local churches not big cathedrals and monasteries. Also, many rich people began to spend money on other 'good works', such as schools, colleges and hospitals. Some paid for 'chantry chapels', where someone prayed for them after they died, to try to get them into heaven. People wanted to have a closer relationship with God. Prayer Books (Books of Hours) helped richer people worship God at home.

With no new groups of monks to join, people wanting to change the Church now found themselves in trouble and persecuted as **heretics**. One group, the 'Lollards', had many supporters but a Lollard revolt against King Henry V was crushed in 1414 and Lollards were punished. But still many poorer people in the towns supported the Lollards. They wanted the Bible in English, not Latin, changes in services and better trained priests who could preach.

In 1414 King Henry V forced all English monasteries to cut their links with foreign monks. From now on they would have to be run by the English. So, while the Church was still important, changes were happening.

NEW WORDS

ECONOMY: Buying and selling. How wealth is made and spent.
HERETICS: people who believe the 'wrong' things.

SOURCE

The brothers shall own nothing, but shall live as pilgrims and strangers in this world, serving God in poverty and humility. They shall beg and not be ashamed, for the Lord Jesus made himself poor in this world for us.

▲ *The rule for how the Franciscan Friars should live, early thirteenth century.*

A story tells of St Francis preaching to the birds. But really he preached to the crows and ravens eating the bodies of dead criminals! He was saying that the Good News about Jesus should be taken to everyone – not just rich people.

SOURCE B

▲ A rich family, the Nevilles, praying. Many rich families spent more time praying together, helped by books of prayers.

Q

1. Make a 'force diagram'. On the left side put reasons why changes happened in the Medieval Church. On the right side put the changes that happened because of these reasons. Link a 'cause' to a 'consequence' with an arrow. Make the arrow *thicker* if you think it was a big change.

2. How could you use the evidence of **Source B** to explain changes in an important area of Church life?

3. Look at **Sources A** and **C**. Why did these people have such different views? Think about when they lived and why this might have made them think so differently.

4. What would you say to the fifteenth century visitor from Venice to explain: a)how the Church was changing, b)why these changes were happening?

SOURCE C

I was a Friar for many a day. But when I saw that how they lived was not how they preached, I threw off my Friar's clothes.

 Written by a Friar who joined the Lollards in about 1400.

What was a Cistercian nun's day like?

YOUR MISSION: to discover what it was like to live a day in the life of a Cistercian nun in about 1200.

Monks and nuns chose to live a life in which they never married, stayed apart from the opposite sex as much as possible, owned nothing, followed strict discipline with few comforts, worked hard and – most important of all – spent most of their day worshipping God. At first, many were children who were given by their families to the monasteries but, after 1100, most were adults who had chosen for themselves. They did this because they believed it would please God and make them more likely to go to heaven.

By the end of the Middle Ages, in about 1500, there were 180 large monasteries in England and Wales and 700 smaller ones. In 1217 there were about 12,500 monks and nuns and this had increased to about 17,500 by 1340. Numbers fell after this, as it became less popular to become a monk or nun, but even so there were still 7,000 monks and nuns when Henry VIII closed the monasteries in the sixteenth century. But what was it like to be a Cistercian nun in 1200, at a place such as Clementhorpe, near York?

NEW WORDS

MASS: service of Holy Communion, when bread and wine is shared to remember Jesus' death.

RULE: written by St Benedict, it explained how a monk, or nun, should live.

SOURCE B

2am, services of the 'Night Office' and 'Lauds of the Dead' – lasted two hours.
Then a time of study.
6am service called 'Prime'.
Then a time of study.
9am short service called 'Terce', followed by **mass**.
Chapter meeting during which a chapter from the **Rule of St Benedict** was read, business discussed, discipline - often a beating - carried out on rule breakers.
Noon, service called 'Sext'.
3pm, service called 'None', followed by mass.
5pm, service called 'Vespers'.
9pm, service called 'Compline'.
Bed and sleep in the common dormitory; the 'great silence'.

▲ *The way a nun's day was organised in summer.*

SOURCE A

▲ *Nuns being led to a service. The men are priests who met with the nuns to lead the service of mass for them. Nuns were not allowed to lead this service. This picture dates from about 1300 and is French.*

SOURCE C

They wear nothing made with furs, or linen. They have two tunics with cowls [hoods] but no additional garments in winter. They sleep in their clothes and never go back to bed after night services. No one misses a service unless they are sick. They never leave the monastery except to work hard. They never speak. They care for strangers and the sick but treat their own bodies very harshly.

▲ *William of Malmesbury describing the life of the Cistercians. William died in 1143.*

SOURCE D

The main and often only meal of the day was usually taken sometime between 11 and 12 o'clock. Throughout the meal a monk, or nun, read a religious book from a raised pulpit built into the wall.

A monk, or nun, was on no account to leave the table, to look around, or make unnecessary signals to others. Above all, absolute silence was to be maintained. To communicate they developed sign language. The nuns at Syon Abbey had over a hundred signs for various types of food; fish was requested by moving the hand sideways; for mustard a sister rubbed her nose with her right hand.

▲ *Stephen Hebron,* Life in a Monastery, *1998.*

SOURCE E

A very solemn service was upon Easter Day, between three and four o'clock in the morning. The church was filled with the smell of incense and a marvellous, beautiful statue of our saviour [Jesus] was held up. The whole choir stood before it with fine flaming torches and many other candles, all singing, rejoicing and praising God.

▲ *A description of the celebration of the Night Office in Durham, at Easter.*

SOURCE F

▲ *The 'night stairs' at Hexham, Northumberland. Stairs led from the dormitory to the church so a person could go straight from sleep to a service.*

INVESTIGATION

You are the investigator!
What was a day like for a Cistercian nun in the spring, or summer of 1200? Write a diary entry describing your day, in which you:

■ explain what makes a person become a nun;
■ describe the way your day is organised around services;
■ describe what services are like;
■ explain whether you are likely to meet any men in the day;
■ describe how you dress, eat, behave – and why.

5 LIVING IN THE COUNTRY

THIS CHAPTER ASKS
What was the Feudal System?
Why did the lives of peasants change in the fourteenth century?
How can we identify a deserted Medieval village?
Are women the forgotten people of Medieval history?

NEW WORDS

MANOR: land owned by a lord.

PEASANT: poor farmer who does not own much land.

TENANT: someone who pays rent, or owes work to pay for their land.

Today, most people live in towns and cities but in the Middle Ages most people lived and worked in the country. In fact, it was not until as late as 1851 that more people in Britain lived in towns and cities than in the countryside. But what was it like living in the country in the Middle Ages?

THE FEUDAL SYSTEM
In Chapters 1 and 2 we have seen how William the Conqueror gave English land, or **manors**, to his chief followers. These powerful landowners were called 'tenants in chief', or 'barons'. In return for this land, they had to provide the king with knights to fight his wars for him. It cost a lot of money to buy the armour, weapons and horses to be a knight. So the barons gave some of their land to their followers and made them knights. These knights could use the money from this land to live well and buy the weapons and equipment they needed as knights. The knights had to fight whenever their barons called them to. They did not do the work on the land; this was done by **peasant** farmers. This is called the 'Feudal System'.

WHAT WAS LIFE LIKE AS A PEASANT?
Hard work! That's the short answer. Some peasants were 'freemen', who could buy and sell land as they wanted to. But most peasants were 'villeins'. The lord controlled their lives.

SOURCE A

A peasant diary from the thirteenth century would be worth all the Pipe Rolls in the Public Records Office.

▲ *Historian H.E.Hallam in,* Life of the People, Agrarian History of England and Wales, 1042 – 1350, 1988. *A 'Pipe Roll' was a government record which listed all the money paid to the king in a year.*

I am your lord. I reward you with lots of land for supporting me. But bring knights to fight for me when I need them.

I am your lord. I reward you with land for supporting me. But come, ready to fight for the king, whenever he calls me to bring knights.

In return for their little plots of land they had to pay the lord to let their daughter marry, when a **tenant** died the best animal had to be given to the lord, they had to pay to grind corn in the lord's mill and make bread in his oven. If they refused they would be fined at the manor court.

Worst of all they had to do unpaid work for the lord. The lord kept some of the land for himself, called demesne land. All the work on this land was done by villeins. All the money went to the lord. Villeins hated this. In the fourteenth century many villeins demanded their freedom. The most famous protest was the Peasants' Revolt, in 1381.

SOURCE B

▲ *Peasants ploughing, in about 1340. Country life was hard.*

SOURCE C

In the twelfth and thirteenth centuries the economy grew and this was reflected in the growth of population, settlement and trade, and rents and prices went up. In contrast rents and prices fell in the late fourteenth and fifteenth centuries and settlements, population and trade all contracted.

▲ *The historian Mark Bailey in Peasant Welfare in England, 1290–1348,* Economic History Review, *1998.*

1. Imagine you are the interviewer for a modern TV chat show. Interview the following people about the Feudal System. For each one ask: How the system afffects their life? What their opinion is of it?

The king.
A baron.
A knight.
A villein.

Write your questions and their imaginary answers.

2. Look at **Source A**. Why do you think this historian wrote this? Does it matter such diaries do not exist?

3. Use **Source C** to explain ways in which life did not stay the same in the country in the Middle Ages.

I am your lord. I will protect you. But you must work for me when I say so and you must pay me taxes

I do all the work and they live in luxury. What a life!

Why did peasants' lives change?

A CHANGING WORLD

Life in the past did not stay the same over centuries. There were often very great changes. In the fourteenth century many peasants were freed from being villeins. But why?

Peasants hated being villeins. Even if they did well and became quite rich they could never be free as long as they were villeins. Their lord could always force them to work for him. If they ran away from the village and were later caught by their lord they could be forced to return.

On Monday June 3rd, 1381, a rich merchant living in Gravesend, Kent, was arrested because he was a runaway villein. It did not matter that he had worked hard in the town and become rich – his lord wanted him back! His friends in the town offered the huge sum of £300 to buy his freedom but his lord refused and he was imprisoned in Rochester Castle. Three days later he was freed when an army of rioters attacked the castle. By this time the whole of Kent and Essex was torn apart by rebellion. But why?

LIFE GETS HARDER

Between 1066 and 1348 peasants had lost a lot of freedom. This was for three main reasons:

- In 1066 the English population was about 2 million. In 1348 it had risen to about 6 million. Poor peasants could not grow enough food for their families. They faced starvation. To survive many agreed to work as villeins.

- With people desperate for food, the price of corn went up. Lords realised they could make a lot of money by forcing villeins to work on the demesne land to produce more corn.

- With so many people and so little land it was hard to protest. It was useless running away from the manor as there was no land to be found elsewhere.

LIFE GETS BETTER?

In 1348 a terrible disease called the **Black Death** arrived in Britain (see Chapter 7). Perhaps a third of the population died. This disaster suddenly meant that those who survived no longer faced starvation. They could take over the land of those who died. They could run away from their manor and find lords with spare land elsewhere. The lack of workers meant lords had to pay more money for work. Between 1311 and 1350 the Bishop of Winchester had paid his workers wages of 2 pennies a day. But by 1390 he had to double the wages to get the work done!

SOURCE A

Are we not all descended from Adam and Eve? But the rich have fine houses and manors, while we must face the wind and rain as we work in the fields. We are called slaves and, if we do not carry out our service [on the lord's land], we are beaten. Let us go to the king and present our complaint to him.

▲ *A speech by the rebel preacher, John Ball. It was recorded by the French writer, Froissart, who visited England soon after the Peasants' revolt.*

The London fish-sellers let the rebels into London because they wanted them to attack the rich merchants who were trying to bring down the price of fish.

SOURCE B

He tried to prove that all men were created equal and that wicked men oppressed others unjustly against God's will. When he had preached this and other madness the people said he should be made archbishop.

▲ *Written shortly afterwards by a monk at St Albans Abbey about John Ball. Rebels with similar ideas to Ball had attacked St Albans Abbey because it made villeins work for nothing on its land.*

With fewer people needing food the price of corn fell and lords lost interest in making villeins work for them. Instead they could make more money by renting their demesne land to peasants and living off the rent money. But some lords tried to stop these changes. They put pressure on the government to pass laws making it illegal to pay higher wages than before. These lords tried to force villeins to stay in the manor and work for them. But now villeins would not accept this. They were ready to revolt!

THE PEASANTS' REVOLT, 1381.

As well as villeins being angry about their lack of freedom, the government was unpopular. War with France was going badly and the king had called for a new tax to pay for it - the Poll Tax. It was unpopular because rich and poor paid the same amount.

On June 2nd, royal tax collectors were murdered in Essex. On June 6th, Rochester Castle was attacked in Kent. The rebels were led by Wat Tyler and a priest named John Ball.

On June 13th the rebels entered London and murdered the Archbishop of Canterbury and many rich merchants. The king was forced to promise to free villeins. But the revolt was crushed and the king broke his promise. Despite this, by 1450 most lords stopped forcing villeins to work for them. Peasants had more freedom than before.

NEW WORDS

BLACK DEATH: the name for the first appearance of a disease called bubonic plague, which first reached Britain in 1348.

SOURCE D

The Holy Church should pay wages to those running each church and the rest be given away. There should be no more villeins but all should be free and equal.

▲ *Wat Tyler's demands to Richard II, according to the Anonimalle Chronicle, written at York shortly after the revolt.*

SOURCE C

▲*Painted about 60 years after the Peasants' Revolt, this picture shows a meeting between Wat Tyler and the king. The Mayor of London kills Tyler and the king turns and calms the peasants by promising to free them.*

Q

1. Design a poster setting out the demands of the rebels in 1381.

2. Look at **Sources B,C,D.** Why might a historian worry about how much these can be trusted as evidence?

3. Using the following headings: population, price of corn, protests, explain why the lives of peasants changed for the worse then for the better.

Discussion Point
What would you do if you disagreed with a law and thought it was wrong?

The village vanishes

YOUR MISSION: to discover whether there was ever a village at the deserted church of Knowlton, Dorset.

At Knowlton, in Dorset, a ruined Medieval church stands alone inside a prehistoric earth circle. There is no village nearby. But was there ever one? And if so, where was it? What can you find out about it? In this Investigation you are an archaeologist on holiday in the area. To find the answers you visit the church, ask the local landowner for permission to explore evidence in a nearby field, search through old documents and modern books. Here is the evidence. But what do you think?

NEW WORDS

HUNDRED: a group of settlements.
KNIGHT'S FEE: an area of land worth enough money to support a knight and his family for a year.
MESSUAGE: a house and land round it.

SOURCE A

▲ *The ruined church of Knowlton, Dorset. Built inside a pre-historic earth circle, it stands on its own with no village near it.*

SOURCE B

Ansger hold two hides from the Earl [of Mortain] in Chenoltone. Ailmer held them in King Edward's time and they were taxed. There is land for one plough there with one slave and one smallholder. There is a mill there worth twelve shillings and six pence. It is all worth twenty-four shillings.

▲ *Domesday Book entry for a place that is probably Knowlton.*

SOURCE C

Giles de Brewosa held this manor and **hundred** until he died, from the Earl of Gloucester. He owed one **knight's fee**. John, his son and heir, is three years old.

▲ *Tax record, 1305.*

SOURCE D

(1) William de Glanvil holds half a fee in Cnolton hundred.
(2) The earls of March held there half a fee which was held by the heirs of Giles de Brewosa.

▲ *Tax record (1) from 1348. Tax record (2) from 1399 and 1425.*

SOURCE E

The Chancel and Nave of the ruined church are of the 12th century; the North Chapel, West Tower and probably the South Porch are of the 15th century; the North Aisle appears to have been added in the 18th century.

   The church was in use in 1550 but few went there by the middle of the 17th century and in 1659 an attempt was made to demolish it; the churchwardens were, however, prevented from doing this. Hutchins [a 19th century writer] records a revival of use about 1730, from which time the North Aisle may come. Later, in the 18th century, the roof fell in and the church was abandoned.

▲ **The Royal Commission on Historical Monuments.**

SOURCE F

Two **messuages**, one garden, one orchard.

▲ *A record from 1594. Knowlton is now reduced to two farms.*

SOURCE G

1667   Samuel and Mary.
1723   Richard of
          Knolton.

▲ *Last baptisms of Knowlton babies at nearby Horton.*

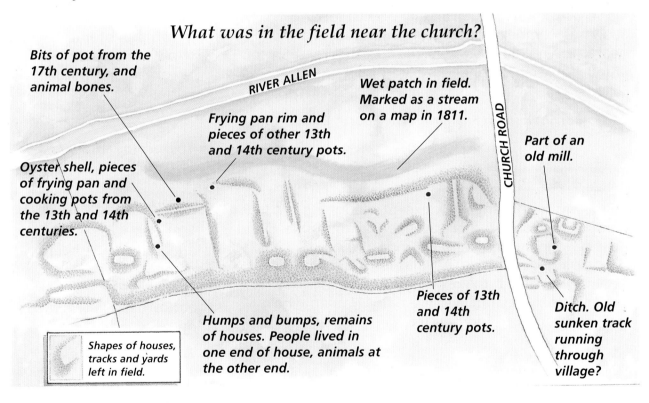

What was in the field near the church?

Bits of pot from the 17th century, and animal bones.

RIVER ALLEN

Frying pan rim and pieces of other 13th and 14th century pots.

Wet patch in field. Marked as a stream on a map in 1811.

CHURCH ROAD

Part of an old mill.

Oyster shell, pieces of frying pan and cooking pots from the 13th and 14th centuries.

Shapes of houses, tracks and yards left in field.

Humps and bumps, remains of houses. People lived in one end of house, animals at the other end.

Pieces of 13th and 14th century pots.

Ditch. Old sunken track running through village?

INVESTIGATION

You are the investigator!
Write your archaeological report.
Include:

■ What made you think Knowlton was strange in the first place.
■ Evidence that there really was a village there once.

■ Where the village was, what evidence survives there, the date people were living there.
■ Clues about when the village started to decline.
■ Whether it was abandoned at once, or probably grew smaller over time.

History or Her-story?

YOUR MISSION: to discover how important a part women played in village life and why it is so difficult to find out about medieval women.

Sometimes it seems that History is all His-story. We hear a lot about men and what they did. But what about Her-story? How important a part did women play in village life?And why is it that men seem to appear so much more than women in the evidence that survives from the Middle Ages? Look at the evidence and decide for yourself.

NEW WORDS

JURORS: group of people who decide the guilt of someone at a trial, or who sort out problems in the village.
PLEDGES: promises to see another person would pay a fine, and be responsible themselves if that person did not.
REEVE: offical elected to look after the village.

SOURCE A

There were sometimes women among the peasantry who were gifted by strength and qualities of leadership and became leaders by force of personality alone, without being given any official job. Agnes Sadler of Romsley, a married woman, headed the peasants who, in 1386, objected to an increase in the labour services demanded by the lord.

▲ *Historian Shulasmith Shahar in,* The Fourth Estate, *1983.*

SOURCE B

There was hardly any work except ploughing for which they were not employed, eg. planting peas and beans, weeding, reaping, binding, threshing, winnowing, thatching. They did much of the sheep shearing. One of the most important of regular servants of the manor was the dairy woman who looked after dairy and poultry.

▲ *Historian Eileen Power in,* Medieval Women, *1975.*

SOURCE C

She hears her child scream, sees the cat eating the bacon and the dog eating the leather, her bread is burning on the fire, her calf is drinking the milk, the pot is running into the fire and her husband is complaining.

▲ *From a Medieval book, called* Holy Maidenhead, *trying to persuade women not to marry but to become nuns instead.*

SOURCE D

Percentage of murderers who were women: 8.4%
Percentage of murder victims who were women: 20.5%

▲ *Thirteenth century figures for English country areas.*

SOURCE E

Percentage of landowners who were women: 14%
Percentage of landowners who were men: 86%

▲ *From a study of ten Midland manors, 1350–1450.*

SOURCE F

In the village the man is in the fields or the woods, everything else is in the woman's hands and it is impossible to ignore this.

▲ *Historian Robert Fossier in* Peasant Life in the Medieval West, *1988.*

INVESTIGATION

SOURCE G

▲ Men and women sharing the farmwork of harvesting, weeding and stone-breaking. From the Luttrell Psalter, 1340.

INVESTIGATION

You are the investigator!
Plan a speech to your class, protesting at the way our view of history in medieval villages seems dominated by men. You will need to justify your complaint by explaining:

■ The kinds of jobs done by women.
■ The importance of these jobs.
■ Things that reduced the power of women.
■ How women still sometimes became leaders.
■ Why men seem to appear more in the surviving records than women. And why this gives a wrong impression of the past.

Discussion Point
Do you think men and women are equal today?

SOURCE H

Farm/household
servants: 114.
Weavers: 96.
Brewers: 39.
Innkeepers: 11.
Nurses: 2.
Farmers: 2.
Dyers: 2.
Fullers: 2
Farrier: 1.
Smith: 1.
Shoe-maker: 1.
Merchant: 1.

▲ Jobs done by women in the Poll Tax returns for the West Riding of Yorkshire, about 1385.

SOURCE I

She remained, as far as the running of her community was concerned, an outsider. On marriage they gave up any independence they had once had. Those who had previously attended courts as tenants now left such business to their husbands. There were no official jobs of responsibility open to them. They did not act as **reeves**, or **jurors** and only occasionally acted as **pledges**.

▲ Historian Henrietta Leyser in, Medieval Women – A Social History of Women in England, 450–1500, 1995.

6 TOWNS IN THE MIDDLE AGES

THIS CHAPTER ASKS

What makes a place a 'town'?
How did towns change in the Middle Ages?
Was it better living in a town or in a village?
Why did towns grow and become more important?

NEW WORDS

BOROUGH: a place with a charter (see below) giving the people living there rights.

BURGHAL PLOTS: long strips of land in a town. People could rent this land. They had a house and shop at one end.

CHARTER: an agreement from a local lord or the king. It gave people living in towns rights and freedoms. They could hold markets weekly, rent land and not have to work for a lord.

FAIRS: large markets. Big towns might have one a year.

WHAT MAKES A PLACE A 'TOWN'?

Today most people in this country live in towns. The biggest towns are called cities. The biggest city today is London – about seven million people live there! In the Middle Ages most people lived in the country. But during the Middle Ages towns grew and became more important. But what is a 'town'? Let's see what a person from the Middle Ages might think, then a modern person.

*A place with land split up into **burghal plots**.*

Where people don't have to work on the lord's land like the villeins do in a village. This gives them free time to make and sell things.

*A place with a market, or even a **fair**.*

Very big ones are run by a council called a 'corporation'.

*A place which has a **borough charter**.*

Groups of craftspeople, called guilds, make rules for how work should be done.

Many different jobs.

Thousands of people live there. Sometimes millions!

Usually has a council to run the place.

Lots of shops.

Lots of places to spend your leisure time.

SOURCE A

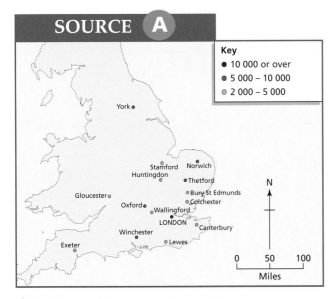

▲ *Main English towns in 1086.*

SOURCE B

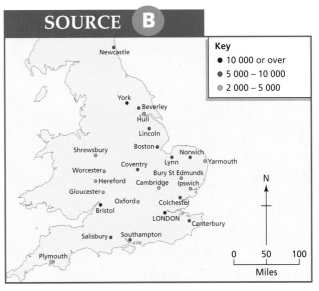

▲ *Main English towns in 1400.*

CHANGING TOWNS

In the Domesday Book (in 1086) there were 111 towns in England. By 1370 there were about 510. Of these, 170 were 'new towns'. Portsmouth was a new town, started in 1194. Liverpool was one, set up in 1207. They had been set up where there had been no town before.

Many towns were not large to start with, but most grew larger as people moved there from the country. One legend tells how Dick Whittington and his cat went to London to make their fortune. Well, there really was a Richard Whittington, who was Mayor of London in the fourteenth century. He came to London from Gloucestershire. Many other people travelled to live in towns too. They found more jobs there and more freedom than in the countryside.

From 1400 onwards more houses in towns began to be made from stone. These newer houses had fireplaces and chimneys to make them more comfortable and safe. But many houses continued to be made from wood. These often caught fire. In fourteenth century Southampton, blacksmiths were banned from the High Street. But fires still happened. Archaeologists there found one house burnt down. In the oven they found the body of a cat that had tried to hide there from the flames. City life could be dangerous.

TOWNS AT THE END OF THE MIDDLE AGES

After 1368 no more new towns were built. The growth of towns slowed down. Some jobs – like the making of cloth – moved out of towns, back to the countryside. This was because there was less freedom in towns than there had once been. The richer townspeople tried to stop new people coming to towns and sharing in their wealth. By 1400 country people had more freedom, and more choice of jobs, too. They had less need to escape to towns.

Q

1. Look at the cartoons. Explain what is similar and different about these two ideas of what makes a place a 'town'.

2. How did towns change during the Middle Ages?

Make notes under these headings:

■ The number of towns.
■ The size of towns.
■ Buildings in towns.
■ Work in towns.
■ The attraction of towns for country people.

So, how much had towns changed – a lot or a little?

Discussion Point
Why do more people today live in cities and towns rather than in the country?

Totnes – A changing medieval town

These two pictures are a modern artist's reconstructions of what Totnes, in Devon, looked like at two points in its history.

Source A shows the town in about 1100.
Source B shows it in about 1400.
They show how the town changed.

Reconstructions like these are based on careful research. The artist checks things found by archaeologists, old descriptions of the town, charters which say when parts of the town were built, and any other evidence that survives today.

NEW WORDS

QUAY: a place where ships land their cargo.

PRIORY: a place where monks spend their lives worshipping God.

FORD: a shallow place where a river can be crossed.

SOURCE A

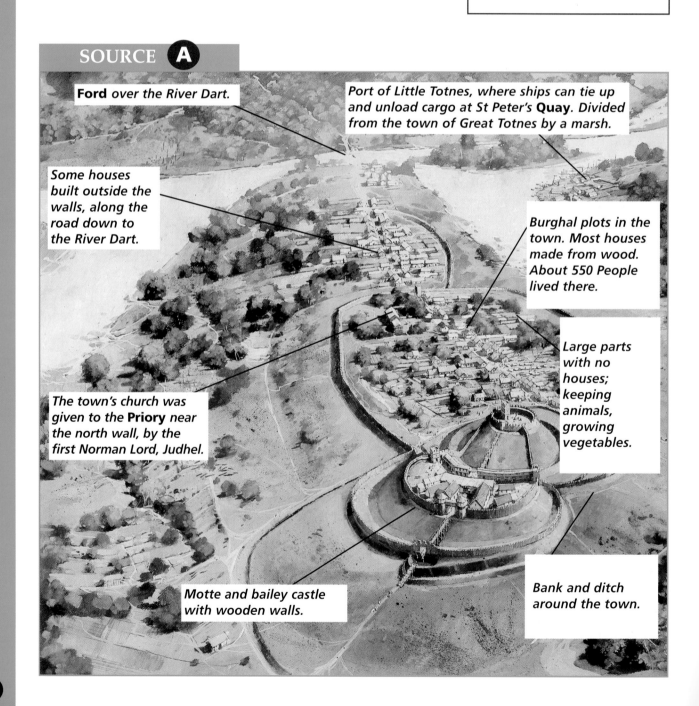

Ford *over the River Dart.*

Port of Little Totnes, where ships can tie up and unload cargo at St Peter's **Quay**. *Divided from the town of Great Totnes by a marsh.*

Some houses built outside the walls, along the road down to the River Dart.

Burghal plots in the town. Most houses made from wood. About 550 People lived there.

The town's church was given to the **Priory** *near the north wall, by the first Norman Lord, Judhel.*

Large parts with no houses; keeping animals, growing vegetables.

Motte and bailey castle with wooden walls.

Bank and ditch around the town.

Q Use these pictures to write a report of how Totnes changed during the Middle Ages. To help you, here are some things to think about:

■ The population of the town.
■ How it is defended.
■ The amount of buildings in the town. What they are made from.
■ The different kinds of buildings in the town.
■ The growth of nearby settlements.
■ How easy it is to travel to the town.

People in towns often did not want to share their wealth with people they thought were 'outsiders'. The charter for Bridgetown, in 1268, was racist and said no Jews were allowed to own land in the town.

SOURCE B

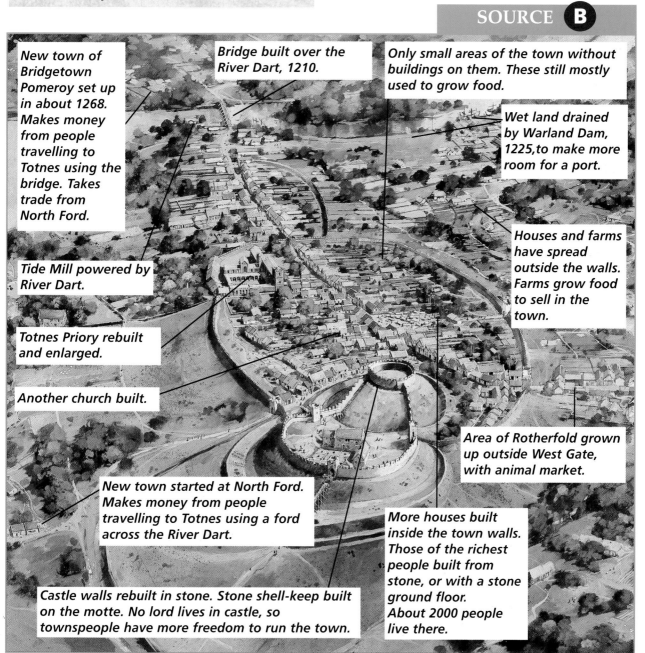

New town of Bridgetown Pomeroy set up in about 1268. Makes money from people travelling to Totnes using the bridge. Takes trade from North Ford.

Bridge built over the River Dart, 1210.

Only small areas of the town without buildings on them. These still mostly used to grow food.

Wet land drained by Warland Dam, 1225, to make more room for a port.

Houses and farms have spread outside the walls. Farms grow food to sell in the town.

Tide Mill powered by River Dart.

Totnes Priory rebuilt and enlarged.

Another church built.

Area of Rotherfold grown up outside West Gate, with animal market.

New town started at North Ford. Makes money from people travelling to Totnes using a ford across the River Dart.

More houses built inside the town walls. Those of the richest people built from stone, or with a stone ground floor. About 2000 people live there.

Castle walls rebuilt in stone. Stone shell-keep built on the motte. No lord lives in castle, so townspeople have more freedom to run the town.

Why did towns become important?

When King Edward I's son was born in 1284, towns were on the mind of the king. The baby was born in Caernarfon – a new town set up by Edward I. When the king wanted to give a present to the baby's nurse he could think of nothing better than a plot of land in this new town! Later, in 1297, the king called together the first ever meeting of **town planners**, to help him rebuild the town of Berwick on the **border** with Scotland. He even wheeled a barrow of earth when Berwick's defences were begun! This is one clue why towns became more important during the Middle Ages. Kings thought they were a good idea. But why? And what other reasons were there?

DIFFERENT REASONS WHY TOWNS BECAME MORE IMPORTANT.

The population was going up during the Middle Ages. This meant there were more people who wanted to buy things. Towns were useful places for buying and selling. Also there were too many people living in the countryside. There were not enough jobs for them there, so many people moved to towns looking for new kinds of work.

Kings and local lords thought they could make money from towns. People would pay rent for a plot of land. Travellers coming to market would pay to visit the town. At markets and fairs, rents were paid for stalls. Often, if someone behaved badly, their punishment was a fine that went to the lord.

During the Middle Ages the rich and powerful wanted to buy **luxury** goods like jewellery and clothes. Many of these were either made in towns, or brought to towns to sell.

Kings and lords found that towns helped them control the countryside. In Wales, English soldiers were put in towns to live. In 1110, the town of Pembroke was set up beside the castle that was already there. The same thing happened at Caernarfon, in 1282. Other towns grew up beside the Yorkshire castles of Pontefract and Richmond. Not all towns had walls, but many built them after 1200. Southampton built its walls after the French attacked the town in 1338. Town walls kept the people living there safe from enemies.

Some towns grew up near places where the king hunted. They supplied him and his followers with things to buy. Others grew up at ports. On the coast, goods were taken in and out of the country through ports like Bristol and Hull.

THINKING IT THROUGH

NEW WORDS

BORDER: where two countries meet.
JUSTICIAR: man in charge of law and order for the king.
LUXURY: items that cost a lot of money.
TOLLS: type of tax paid by travellers.
TOWN PLANNER: a person skilled at setting up new towns.

SOURCE A

The Bishop of Lincoln has built a row of houses in the middle of the market place. So that he will get more rent.

▲ *An account from 1279 about the town of New Thame.*

WHERE A TOWN MIGHT GROW:

- On a good road where many people travelled.
- At a place where roads joined, or crossed.
- Where a road crossed a river, or was near a river.

Baldock, in Hertfordshire, takes its name from the Medieval word for Baghdad, capital of modern Iraq! When it was set up, in 1168, it was hoped it too would become rich and famous.

SOURCE B

An early map, from about 1600, showing the town of Conwy, Wales. It clearly shows how the town was protected by the nearby castle and a town wall.

SOURCE C

There are famous criminals and thieves at a place called Penthlyn. The **Justiciar** is pleased to agree to setting up a town of merchants.

 From the charter setting up the town of Bala in Wales, 1324.

SOURCE D

A man, no matter how rich he is, who lives there for a year and a day without being challenged shall be free.

From the charter for Haverford West, about 1200.

SOURCE E

They will not have to pay any **tolls** wherever they travel in the land and in the seaports.

 Rights given to the people of Devizes, in 1142.

SOURCE F

The king's men lived too far from his [hunting] manor. So the king gave land to men who would come and build and gave them a market.

 A record, from 1279, of why New Woodstock was set up.

Q **1.** You are one of the town planners called to the meeting in 1297. After the meeting the king has told you to let people across the country know why towns are so useful. As many people cannot read, you need to use both pictures and words. Design a strip cartoon with each box explaining a different reason why a town is useful.

2. Look at the **Sources A–F**. Each one illustrates a different 'cause' of why towns grew and became more important during the Middle Ages. For each source, explain what reason it gives you for why towns grew. Are any sources similar? If so, which?

3. Which of the reasons (in **answer 2.**) do you think was most important? Compare it with the other reasons. Explain why your 'top reason' is most important.

On the move

YOUR MISSION: to help the Bishop of Salisbury decide where to build a 'new town'.

It is 1218 and the Bishop of Salisbury, Richard Poore, has a problem. His cathedral is high up on a hill at Old Sarum, in Wiltshire. He wants to move it! At the same time he wants to build a completely new town next to his new cathedral. A new town will make money for the Church.

The bishop has turned to you for help. You are his archdeacon and help him run his lands and churches. He wants a full report from you, which identifies all the problems of staying where he is. He wants you to decide where he should move to and how this will solve the problems that he is facing at the moment. He wants to move to a place where his new town will be free to grow.

NEW WORDS

CASTELLAN: servant of the king, in charge of a royal castle.

GLARE: bright reflection.

SOURCE A

Let us descend joyfully to the plains, where the valley abounds in corn, where the fields are beautiful and where there is freedom from oppression.

▲ *Written in about 1199 by Peter of Blois.*

SOURCE C

When King Stephen landed in England he held his council at Oxford and arrested the Bishop of Salisbury and his nephews. He put them in prison until they had surrendered their castles.

▲ *From the Anglo-Saxon Chronicle, 1137. It tells how 80 years earlier the king had taken over the running of Old Sarum castle from the person who was then bishop.*

SOURCE B

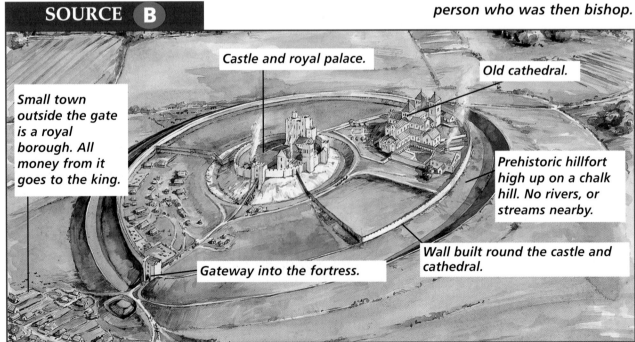

Castle and royal palace.

Old cathedral.

Small town outside the gate is a royal borough. All money from it goes to the king.

Prehistoric hillfort high up on a chalk hill. No rivers, or streams nearby.

Gateway into the fortress.

Wall built round the castle and cathedral.

▲ *Modern artist's picture of what Old Sarum would have looked like before the cathedral moved.*

SOURCE D

We are dominated and oppressed by the **castellan** and soldiers in the castle. We are not allowed to go in and out without permission from the castle. The faithful are not allowed to visit the church. The wind around the hill is so loud we can hardly hear each other sing. The place gives us colds in the head. The church is shaken by winds and storm. The place has no trees and grass and the **glare** from the chalk has blinded some priests. Water has to be brought a great distance and costs a lot.

▲ *From a complaint sent from the cathedral at Old Sarum to the pope, in Rome, in 1217. The priests who wrote it wanted the pope to agree to their request to move. They listed as many problems as they could think of.*

SOURCE E

Like the mountains of Gilboa, without rain, dew, flowers or grass, where no nightingale sings. There was a shortage of water and a tiring climb to the top of the hill.

▲ *Written by Henry of Avranches about the time of the move. He was a priest and wanted to compare Old Sarum with somewhere in the Bible. He deliberately chose the worst place he could think of, to try to show how bad Old Sarum was.*

INVESTIGATION

You are the investigator!

You are the archdeacon with the task of advising the bishop on where to build his new town. Write a report in which you:

- Describe all the problems of staying where you are.
- Explain why setting up a new cathedral and new town might solve the problems.
- If you find any weaknesses with any of the evidence you are using, you need to explain why.
- Look at the map below. Choose the best site for building the new town. Explain why this is the best site.

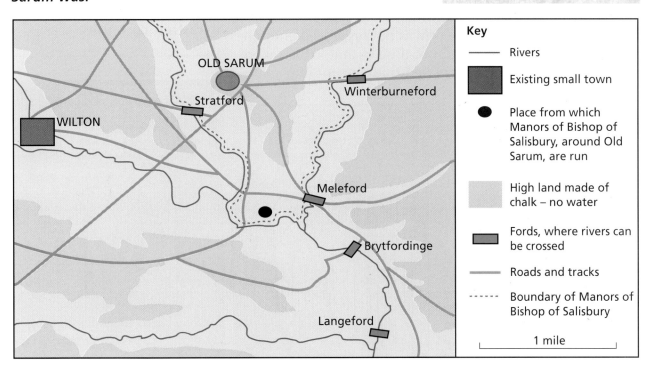

Key

— Rivers

■ Existing small town

● Place from which Manors of Bishop of Salisbury, around Old Sarum, are run

High land made of chalk – no water

▬ Fords, where rivers can be crossed

— Roads and tracks

----- Boundary of Manors of Bishop of Salisbury

1 mile

7 HEALTH AND MEDICINE IN THE MIDDLE AGES

THIS CHAPTER ASKS
Why did so many people die from diseases?
What was thought to cause disease?
Was there any progress in the way disease was treated in the Middle Ages?

WHY WAS LIFE UNHEALTHY?
People living in the Middle Ages could not expect to live as long as people live today. The **life expectancy** of a man born today is about 71 years. A woman can expect to live on average for about 80 years. A man could expect to live on average less than 40 years in the Middle Ages. Women usually had even shorter lives. This was because many women died while giving birth, or soon afterwards.

Many people living in Britain died from killer diseases such as bubonic plague, measles, smallpox, syphilis (called the 'French Pox') and typhus. Some of these, such as bubonic plague, swept across the country every few years after 1348 in what are called **epidemics**. In these plague years many thousands of people died.

WHY DID DISEASES SPREAD?
In the Middle Ages towns grew in size. Crowding people together made it easier for diseases to spread. To make matters worse, these towns were often very dirty. People often caught diseases from drinking dirty water, or from rats and fleas. The government was not organised enough to clean up towns, although from time to time efforts were made to improve things. Increased **trade** meant that some people travelled to distant countries. When they returned home they often brought back new diseases with them! Warfare also meant that armies often carried diseases from one place to another.

A fourteenth century painting called 'The three living and the three dead'. It is a Christian painting reminding people that, no matter who they are, they must one day die. It is the will of God. ➤

NEW WORDS
ASTROLOGY: the belief that people's lives are affected by the stars and planets.
CAESARIAN BIRTH: an operation on a woman to remove a baby.
EPIDEMIC: when many people catch a disease.
HUMOURS: the Greek and Roman idea that there are 4 substances in a human body: blood, yellow bile, black bile, phlegm. People thought they would get sick if there was too much of one of these in the body.
LIFE EXPECTANCY: the average number of years a person can expect to live.
TRADE: buying and selling. It often involved travel by merchants to distant countries.

SOURCE A

SOURCE B

Merchants loading a ship. ➤

In fourteenth century London a man, named Roger, filled his cellar with human waste. Unfortunately, he fell through the rotten floorboards in his house and drowned!

SOURCE C

▲ *A picture drawn in 1375 showing a* **caesarian** *birth.*

HOW WERE DISEASES TREATED?

Many people thought diseases were a punishment sent from God. To stop disease they thought that sick people should pray and try to live better lives. Others believed in the ancient Greek and Roman idea that inside people's bodies were substances called **humours**. They thought disease was caused when there was too much of one of these substances in a person's body. To make people better they cut their bodies to let blood flow out. Some thought that the stars and planets affected life; this idea is known as **astrology**. They thought people could only be treated if the planets were in the 'right' position. Other people thought herbs and spices could cure disease. Yet others believed in magic spells.

Many people died after operations because there were no pain killers, or because surgeons' hands and knives were dirty. Medieval people did not know that disease is caused by germs because they did not have modern microscopes.

Q

1. Make two Spidergrams, one to record 'Why diseases spread' and the other to record 'Different ideas about treating disease.'

2. Look at **Source C**. Why would this mother probably have died in the Middle Ages?

3. What might the person who painted **Source A** have thought about disease?

4. **Source B** shows nothing about disease but it is important evidence which explains why disease spread! Why?

5. Why was life so unhealthy in the Middle Ages?

Mention:

■ Evidence which shows this (e.g. how long people lived).
■ How different things caused disease to spread and then made it hard to treat.
■ Your opinion on the main reason life was unhealthy and why you think this.

Discussion Point
What could you do to make your lifestyle healthier?

Was there progress in medicine?

CHANGE OVER FOUR HUNDRED YEARS

We are looking at history between AD1066 and about 1500. This is over four hundred years. This is a long time and during this period people's ideas about disease and medicine changed.

'CHANGE' AND 'PROGRESS'

'Change' is not the same as 'progress'. 'Change' means that things are just different. Changes may be good, or bad. 'Progress' involves changes which make things better. They are changes which improve things. Many ideas about health and medicine changed in the Middle Ages. But did they make things better? Or worse? Were they 'progress'? Look at the evidence and see what you think!

THINGS THAT STAYED THE SAME

Some things did not change at all in the Middle Ages. People did not discover that germs cause diseases. This did not happen until the nineteenth century. This made it hard to stop diseases spreading, or stop wounds from getting infected. Most towns and cities continued to be dirty and unhealthy places.

THINGS THAT CHANGED

- Greek and Roman ideas about humours became better known after the twelfth century. Doctors came to believe in these ideas even though they were wrong.

- New drugs and spices reached Europe in the thirteenth century. But many medicines made from them did not cure people.

- Education improved. People began to study human bodies carefully and the way different diseases affected people. From the fourteenth century, doctors were allowed to cut up dead bodies. This helped them see how the body works.

- The Christian Church set up more hospitals in the fourteenth and fifteenth centuries. But they were mostly places for the sick to rest, as people were unsure what caused disease.

- Operations became more complicated. Surgeons used new instruments. But many people still died because germs got into their wounds from dirty knives.

CRUSADES: wars in the Middle East, between Christians and Muslims.

Princess Elizabeth of Hungary became a nun in 1227. She set up a hospital for poor, sick people. A legend says she was so keen to serve the poor that she drank the water used to clean the blood and pus from their bodies. After she died, Elizabeth was made a saint.

Christian nuns in a fifteenth-century hospital. Many Christian hospitals were set up in the fourteenth and fifteenth centuries. ▼

SOURCE A

50

SOURCE B

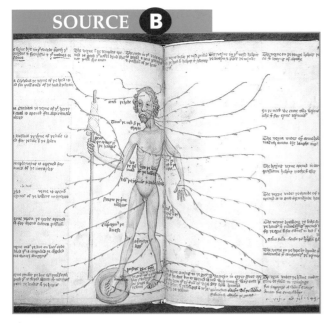

▲ *Book showing where blood could be drained. This Greek idea of humours came from the Middle East.*

WHY DID CHANGES HAPPEN?

■ More trade meant that new herbs, spices and drugs were brought to Europe.

■ Inventions of new tools helped improve operations.

■ The Church lost some of its power over education. The Church then found it hard to stop the cutting up of dead bodies, which it thought was wrong.

■ Knights fighting in the **Crusades** in the Middle East brought Arab ideas back to Europe. These contained Greek and Roman ideas about humours which had been lost in Western Europe since Roman times.

■ There were more monks and nuns and many of them helped to run hospitals.

SOURCE C

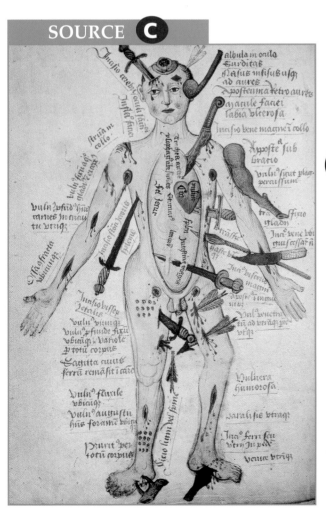

◄ *A picture from the fourteenth century showing wounds and how to treat them. Doctors could decide how to treat different injuries because, by this time, they had more knowledge about how the human body works.*

Q

1. In your own words, explain the difference between 'change' and 'progress'.

2. Look at THINGS THAT CHANGED. Use the information on this page to explain why each change happened.

3. a Choose one source which you think shows 'change' that led to 'progress' in ideas about health and medicine.

b Then choose one which did not lead to 'progress'. For each one, explain why you decided to choose it.

4. Look at all the evidence. How much 'progress' do you think there was in medicine in the Middle Ages?

The Black Death, 1348

SOURCE A

◀ This fourteenth century picture shows 'death' striking down people with the Black Death. The artist has painted 'death' blindfolded, to show that the disease killed people without caring who they were. The idea behind the painting is that God has sent death.

SOURCE B

To the Lord Mayor of London: Quickly remove all filth lying in the streets and lanes of the city. Have it taken far away. Have the city and the surrounding area cleaned from all smells and to be kept clean. This will stop the smell from causing any more deaths. The smells are now so foul that day and night the air is infected and the city is poisoned to the danger of men.

▲ From a letter sent from the English King Edward III in 1349. This was a year after the Black Death arrived in England.

YOUR MISSION: to report why people were unable to stop the Black Death from spreading.

THE BLACK DEATH

This was the most terrible disease of the Middle Ages. The official name of the disease is bubonic plague. It killed perhaps one in every three people when it first reached Europe in the fourteenth century.

WHEN DID IT APPEAR?

It first reached Europe in 1347. It had started in Asia and spread. It had been carried on ships.

HOW DID IT SPREAD?

Rats carried the plague in their blood. Fleas carried it to people when they bit them. Rubbish in the streets encouraged rats. Many rats lived close to people and burrowed into houses. It was easy for their fleas to jump onto people.

SCARED PEOPLE AND DIFFERENT IDEAS

In 1348 people were scared! They did not know what was causing the Black Death. They had lots of ideas. But no one could stop the disease. When this disease first reached Europe, writers and artists recorded their ideas about it. By looking at this evidence we can find out more about what people in the Middle Ages thought caused disease.

A report written by the University of Paris in 1348. ➤

SOURCE C

On March 20th, 1345 the planets Saturn, Jupiter and Mars joined together. The joining together of Saturn and Mars caused death and disaster. The joining together of Mars and Jupiter spread plague in the air.

SOURCE D

Rabbi Jacob sent me a leather bag. In it was red and black powder. I was ordered to throw this powder into the wells.

▲ These are the words of a Jew named Balavignus. He is 'confessing' that the Jews were spreading the Black Death by putting poison into drinking wells. He was tortured until he 'confessed'.

SOURCE E

God often allows plagues, miserable famines, wars and other kinds of suffering to happen. He uses them to punish men and to stop their sins. The plague has attacked England because so many people have been proud and rotten in their lives.

▲ From a letter written by the monk in charge of Christchurch Abbey, Canterbury, to the Bishop of London. It was written in September 1348.

THE GREATEST KILLER OF THE MIDDLE AGES

The Black Death first arrived in England, in Dorset, in the summer of 1348. By the middle of August it had reached Bristol. From the West Country it spread across Britain killing thousands of people. It reappeared several times between then and the end of the seventeenth century. Each time it killed great numbers of people. No one knew what caused it and it was harder to discover the cause because it could affect people in three different ways: boils in the groin and armpits; blood poisoning; and in the lungs, causing terrible coughing. These seemed like three different diseases.

SOURCE F

▲ These men were called Flagellants. They believed that the Black Death was sent by God to punish people for their sins (things they had done wrong). They whipped themselves because they thought that God would forgive people and stop sending the disease.

INVESTIGATION

You are the investigator!

You are a modern doctor. You are investigating why people in 1348 could not stop the Black Death from spreading. You will need to look at the evidence and write your report.

In your report:

- Explain what we now know really caused the disease.
- Describe the ideas people had in 1348 about what caused it.
- Decide how reliable you think these ideas were and why.
- From your investigation: Why were people in 1348 unable to stop the Black Death?

THIS CHAPTER ASKS

How did England get on with its neighbours?
Why was England the most powerful country in Britain?
Owain Glyndwr: 'Prince of Wales', or traitor?

NEW WORDS

OVERLORD: the king who had the final control over another ruler. An overlord often had the right to take taxes from other rulers.
REALM: a country ruled by a king, a prince, or queen.

Today there are only two separate countries in the British Isles. One of them – the United Kindom – is made up of England, Scotland, Wales and Northern Ireland. The other country is the Irish Republic, which makes up the rest of the island of Ireland. In the early Middle Ages things were different. England, Scotland, Wales and Ireland were different countries, or **realms**.

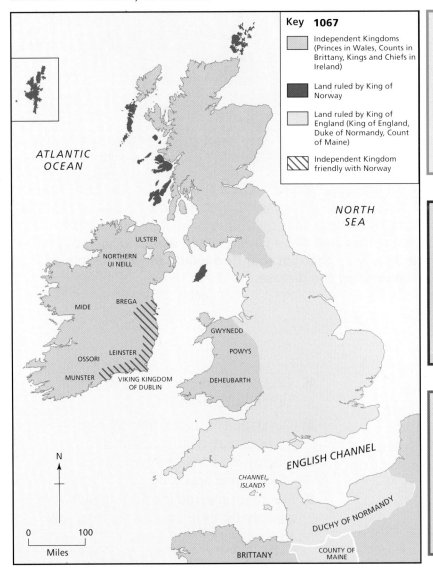

Key 1067

Independent Kingdoms (Princes in Wales, Counts in Brittany, Kings and Chiefs in Ireland)

Land ruled by King of Norway

Land ruled by King of England (King of England, Duke of Normandy, Count of Maine)

Independent Kingdom friendly with Norway

ATLANTIC OCEAN

NORTH SEA

ULSTER
NORTHERN UI NEILL
MIDE
BREGA
OSSORI
LEINSTER
MUNSTER
VIKING KINGDOM OF DUBLIN

GWYNEDD
POWYS
DEHEUBARTH

ENGLISH CHANNEL

CHANNEL ISLANDS

DUCHY OF NORMANDY

BRITTANY
COUNTY OF MAINE

N

0   100
Miles

Ireland

1169, Norman, Strongbow, helps King of South Leinster, regain his throne.
1171, Strongbow tries to make himself king.

Wales

1067–75, Norman lords seize lan in east and south Wales.
1135–54, Welsh push them back.
1267, Henry III of England recognises Llewellyn, Prince of Gwynedd, as Prince of all Wales.

Scotland

1174, Henry II of England makes king of Scots accept English king as his overlord.
1296, Edward I of England invao Scotland. Scots revolt, led by Wi Wallace. Edward captures and k

Q

1. In what ways was Britain different in 1500 compared with 1067?

2. Choose either: Scotland, Wales, or Ireland. Explain how its relationship with England changed in the Middle Ages.

Discussion Point
What groups of people in Britain today sometimes face discrimination? How could this be prevented?

England and Scotland had their own kings. Wales was split up and ruled by different princes. Ireland was divided up between a number of different chiefs and kings. During the Middle Ages the relationship between these countries changed. The two maps in THE BIG PICTURE tell you what Britain was like at the beginning and the end of the Middle Ages. The trackways between the two maps show what happened in the relationship between England and its neighbours in this time.

When Edward I captured Robert the Bruce's wife and sisters, he kept them in cages hung on the outside of the castle walls at Berwick.

1171, Henry II of England invades Ireland to stop Strongbow. Irish accept Henry as overlord.
15th Century, English only control small parts of Ireland.

1277–83, Edward I of England invades Wales, kills Llewellyn, builds castles and towns. Welsh not allowed important jobs.
1400–08, revolt of Owain Glyndwr. Defeated.

Wallace.
1306–28, Scots revolt, led by Robert the Bruce. Bruce defeats Edward II at Bannockburn, 1314.

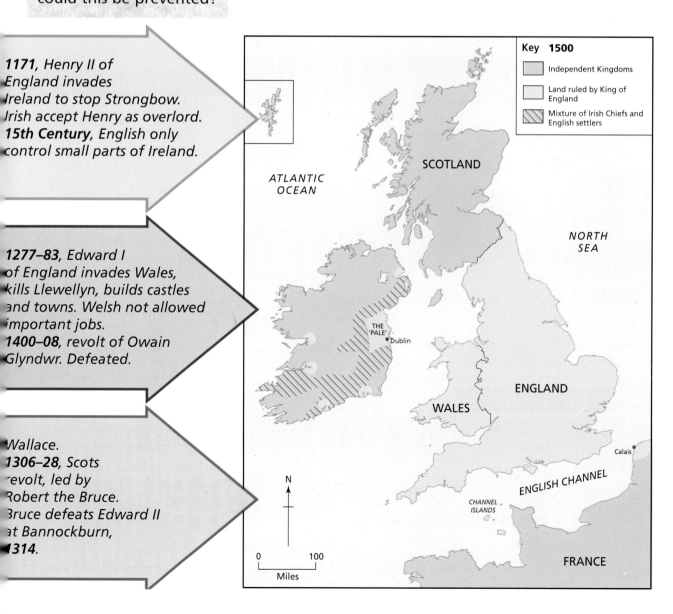

Key 1500
Independent Kingdoms
Land ruled by King of England
Mixture of Irish Chiefs and English settlers

ATLANTIC OCEAN · SCOTLAND · NORTH SEA · THE 'PALE' · Dublin · ENGLAND · WALES · Calais · ENGLISH CHANNEL · CHANNEL ISLANDS · FRANCE

N · 0 100 Miles

Why was England powerful?

YOUR MISSION: to discover why England was more powerful than its neighbours. And whether this meant it could always make them obey the English.

NEW WORDS

MILITARY TECHNOLOGY: Ways of fighting and weapons used in war. The Normans used well armed knights and these could often defeat less well armed foot soldiers.
TANNING: treating skin in a way that turns it into leather. This is usually done with animal skin.

SOURCE A

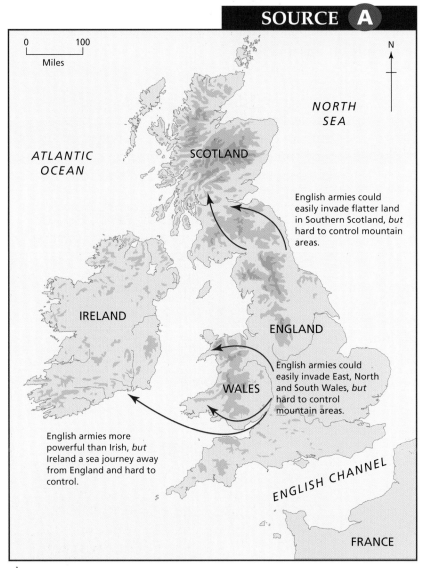

English armies could easily invade flatter land in Southern Scotland, *but* hard to control mountain areas.

English armies could easily invade East, North and South Wales, *but* hard to control mountain areas.

English armies more powerful than Irish, *but* Ireland a sea journey away from England and hard to control.

▲ *English power and problems.*

SOURCE B

1150	England Ireland	2½ million. 500,000
1250	England Wales	4 million. 300,000.
1300	England Scotland	5 million. 500,000.

▲ The population of England and its neighbours at the time of the main English invasions.

SOURCE C

Entering into alliances with some Irish chieftains the Normans seized land and cattle from others. They built great castles as they penetrated, with their superior **military technology**, into all parts of Ireland except western and central Ulster. And yet they eventually became part of the traditional Irish pattern of warring tribes. They married Irish, changed their Norman-French language for Irish, adopting Irish ways and Irish laws. Many Normans became 'more Irish than the Irish'.

▲ The historian Robert Kee in the book, Ireland, 1980.

SOURCE D

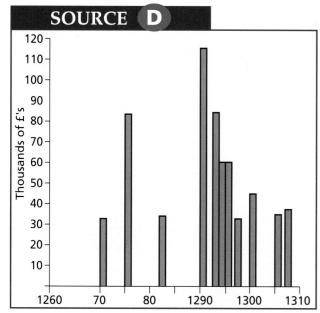

▲ *Graph showing special taxes which the English Parliament agreed that the king should collect between 1260 and 1310. This huge amount of money helped the English fight wars in Wales, Scotland and France. The English king could collect this money because England was such a rich country growing many crops, selling wool, trading in the growing towns.*

SOURCE E

The Norman barons were successful because Wales and Ireland were ruled by rival warring princes and kings who could produce only limited resistance. But Scotland had already developed into a relatively unified, powerful kingdom before any Norman appeared in the British isles.

▲ *The historian Alexander Grant in* **The Making of Britain,** *1985.*

SOURCE F

For the English, winning battles against the Scots was almost always easy. But the problems of conquering and then controlling from London, a country which was so far away and difficult to reach was impossible to solve.

▲ **Historical Atlas of Britain,** *1981.*

INVESTIGATION

You are the investigator!

You are a modern historian trying to discover why England was more powerful than its neighbours in Britain in the Middle Ages. To write your report you will need to:

■ From what you know from the BIG PICTURE explain the ways that England had an impact on the lives of the nearby countries.

■ Look at the evidence in this INVESTIGATION and sort it into: things about England that made England strong; things about its neighbours that made them weaker than England.

In 1297 the Scot, William Wallace, defeated the English at the battle of Stirling Bridge. The Scots killed the English Treasurer, Cressingham, skinned him and **tanned** his skin to make sword belts.

■ Decide whether England was always able to do what it wanted to its neighbours, or whether things were sometimes more complicated.

Owain Glyndwr – 'Prince', or traitor?

YOUR MISSION: how did Owain Glyndwr try to present himself as the true 'Prince of Wales'.

In 1400 a Welsh landowner named Owain Glyndwr led a revolt against the English King, Henry IV. Over a century before this, in 1283, the English king, Edward I, had conquered the last ruler of Wales, Llewellyn. Following this English victory, Wales had been under the control of the English. The English built castles to keep the Welsh from rebelling, built towns that the Welsh were not allowed to live in, stopped Welsh people from using the English law courts in Wales, took land from many of the leading people in Wales. In 1301 King Edward had made his own son Prince of Wales. From that time on, the eldest son of the ruler of England has always had the **title** 'Prince of Wales'.

Many Welsh people hated the English. When Owain rose in revolt they joined him in the hope of driving out the English. Owain took the title 'Prince of Wales' and claimed that he was the true ruler of the Welsh. His revolt lasted until 1409. Although he was defeated he was never captured by the English. He escaped into the mountains and the Welsh would not betray him to the English. No one knows when he died. No one knows where he is buried. Before he was defeated Owain tried many ways to show that he was the true 'Prince of Wales' and not a traitor.

NEW WORDS

COAT OF ARMS: badge of a high ranking person.
FOUNDED: to start, to begin something.
TITLE: a rank like 'prince', or 'king'.

SOURCE B

He is of the family of Lord Rhys and of the family of Bleddyn ap Cynfyn.

▲ *Written about Owain by the Welsh poet, Iolo Goch, in about 1390. Iolo was a supporter of Owain. Lord Rhys had been a powerful ruler of the Welsh princedom of Deheubarth and died in 1197. Bleddyn had **founded** the Welsh princedom of Powys and had died in 1075. Iolo wanted to show that Owain descended from the Welsh royal families who had ruled Wales before the English conquest.*

SOURCE A

> *A piece of horse-harness, found at Harlech castle, in western Wales. It shows the badge of Owain. He had taken this badge from the **coat of arms** of the rulers of Gwynedd. It was a member of this royal family who had united Wales in the thirteenth century and been the last Welsh Prince of Wales.*

SOURCE C

He was like a light shining in battle, his only delight was to ride war-horses.

▲ *A Welsh poem about Owain.*

SOURCE D

Brutus, your most noble ancestor and mine was the first crowned king who lived in England which was once called Great Britain. Brutus had three sons. You are descended from one named Albanactus. The descendants of another, ruled until the last of their family, named Cadwaladr, died. I, dear cousin, am descended directly from Cadwaladr.

▲ *From a letter written by Owain to the King of Scotland in about 1402. He is claiming that both he and the king of Scotland were related to ancient heroes of the past. These ancient heroes we now know were imaginary people but at the time of Owain many people believed they had really existed.*

SOURCE E

Owain and his wild followers, even when defeated, copied the ways royalty live. He also held, or pretended to hold, a parliament at Machynlleth.

▲ *From the Chronicle of Adam of Usk. Adam was a friend of one of Owain's supporters but tried to hide this in his writings. Although he was Welsh, he wrote some years after Owain's death and he was not in Wales at the time of Owain, but was living in Rome.*

SOURCE F

Owain Glyndwr has called a parliament to meet at Harlech. Four of the most important people in each local area of Wales will attend it.

▲ *From a letter written in 1405, to the English king, Henry IV, by John Stanley one of his trusted servants. Stanley lived on the border of Wales and got his information from two powerful Welshmen who were trusted by Owain.*

SOURCE G

The only head of Wales, or the Welsh...
Owain, by the grace of God, Prince of Wales...

▲ *Titles used by Owain about himself. The first was used before his revolt. The second was used in 1404, after he had started his revolt.*

SOURCE H

If, as time goes by, it appears to the three lords that they are the people mentioned by the prophet who will divide and rule Great Britain, then they will work, together and alone, to do the best they can to see that this is done.

▲ *This was written in 1405, when Owain was working with two other enemies of Henry IV to split up and rule England and Wales. These were Henry Percy, Earl of Northumberland and Edmund Mortimer. They were powerful English lords. Owain believed this had been written about long ago by Merlin who was thought to be able to tell the future.*

INVESTIGATION

You are the investigator!

You are an agent working for the English king, Henry IV. Your job is to report on how Owain Glyndwr is trying to present himself as the real 'Prince of Wales'. You, of course, think he is just a traitor!

■ Look at each source and say how each reveals a way that Owain is claiming to be a true Prince.
■ Decide how useful and reliable each piece of evidence is.
■ Which of these attempts by Owain do you think is most dangerous?

9 WAR AND SOCIETY

THIS CHAPTER ASKS

In what ways did war affect people's lives?
How and why did warfare change in the Middle Ages?
Why did the Hundred Years War last so long?
What was the impact of the Wars of the Roses on England?
Why did King Richard III lose the battle of Bosworth?

NEW WORDS

ARMOUR: the metal protection for a knight's body.
PLATE ARMOUR: was made from sheets of strong metal.
LOOTING: stealing from conquered people.
RANSOMS: money paid by captured knights to their captors to let them go free.
SOCIETY: the way in which people live together and have an impact on each other's lives.

WAR IN THE MIDDLE AGES

There were many wars in the Middle Ages: the Normans used violence to conquer England; powerful barons sometimes fought against the king; different members of the royal family sometimes fought each other for the right to rule; England fought wars against neighbouring countries. Many people thought a 'good' king was one powerful enough to conquer and take wealth from other countries.

This does not mean there was always fighting going on. There were many years of peace. Often wars were fought between the rich and powerful, and ordinary people just got on with their own lives. Often, for English people at least, the violence was happening in somebody else's country.

WAR AND THE LIVES OF ORDINARY PEOPLE

But war often did have an impact on people's lives. Here are some of the ways that warfare affected society.

It took a lot of weapons to fight a big battle. In 1346 the English archers who defeated the French at the battle of Crecy were supplied with over 12,000 arrows.

SOURCE A

The feudal system made peasants pay for a knight's equipment.

Wars against Wales, Scotland and France cost a lot of money. Kings had to call parliaments to agree to taxes.

Conquered land was given as rewards to the king's supporters.

As countries fought each other they became more united and more aware of what made them different to their enemies. They began to think of themselves as 'English', 'Scottish', 'Welsh', 'French'...

Soldiers made money from looting and from ransoms.

It was hard to trade when it was not safe to travel.

Whole areas were sometimes destroyed. But some people made money supplying armour, weapons and ships for war.

CHANGING WARFARE

Between 1066 and 1500 many changes took place in how wars were organised, fought and paid for.

At first Medieval armies were 'feudal armies'. The knights and foot-soldiers were sent by the barons who had received land from the king. The king did not pay them for fighting for him. But these armies were often not well trained or experienced. By 1330 this had totally changed. The king paid full-time soldiers wages to fight. Some were knights but many were archers and foot-soldiers. These armies were more skilful but expensive!

Armour and weapons changed too. Chain-mail was replaced by **plate armour**. This gave better protection but was more expensive. In 1350 the equipment of a soldier cost eight times the amount it had cost only 50 years before. Even so, knights could still be killed if they were knocked to the ground. Foot-soldiers carried little knives called misericords to stab into gaps in the armour, or through eyeholes in helmets. The name means kind hearted, because the soldiers were giving the knights a rest [from life!]. It was a medieval joke. Although Knights did not think it was very funny! By the end of the Middle Ages cannons were being used to attack castles. These cost a lot of money too.

Q

1. Look at the two knights. Explain the ways in which they are similar/different.

2. Make a table with two columns entitled: *'Ways wars improved the lives of some people'* and *'Ways wars harmed the lives of some people'*. Complete the table using this BIG PICTURE.

3. Imagine you are an English ruler in about 1450. Describe how warfare has changed over the Middle Ages, explain the problems this causes you and how you try to solve these problems.

SOURCE B

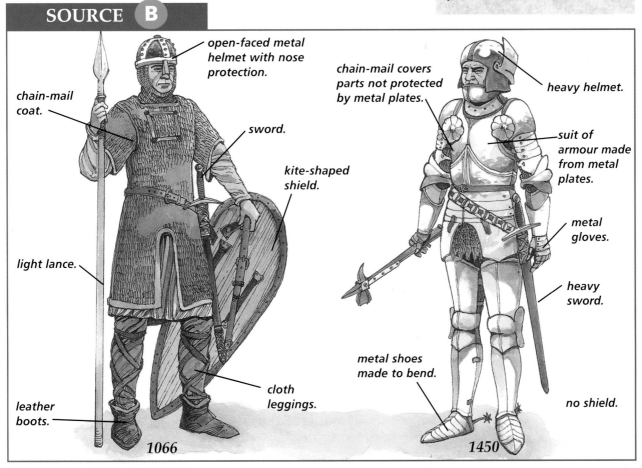

- open-faced metal helmet with nose protection.
- chain-mail coat.
- sword.
- kite-shaped shield.
- light lance.
- leather boots.
- cloth leggings.

1066

- chain-mail covers parts not protected by metal plates.
- heavy helmet.
- suit of armour made from metal plates.
- metal gloves.
- heavy sword.
- metal shoes made to bend.
- no shield.

1450

The Hundred Years War

THINGS ARE NOT ALWAYS HOW THEY SEEM

Many people remember this as a war in which the English won many great victories over the French. But did it really last a hundred years? Why did it last so long? And if England won so many famous victories why did the French succeed in finally defeating the English?

THE HUNDRED YEARS WAR

This name was first used by historians in the early nineteenth century. It describes wars fought between England and France between 1337 and 1453. In 1337 King Edward III of England claimed he also had the right to rule France. Although he gave up this claim in 1360, it was the start of a series of English attacks on France. In 1346 he won a great victory over the French at Crecy. In 1356 his son, the Black Prince, defeated the French at the battle of Poitiers. French knights were slaughtered by English and Welsh archers.

At Poitiers, King John of France was captured by the English. It cost him over £250,000 to buy back his freedom. This was a vast amount of money – over three times the amount that Edward III normally spent in a year. Edward used a lot of the money to rebuild Windsor Castle. But after 1369 the English won few victories; Edward and his son died. The new king –Richard II – was a boy.

In 1415 the English attacked again. This time they were led by King Henry V. He was a clever and skilful king and general. Once more he claimed the right to rule France. In 1415 he won a huge victory at Agincourt. By 1422 he had conquered much of France. In 1422 he died and his eight month old baby son, Henry VI, became king of both lands. The French fought back and united against the English. They were led by Joan of Arc, who claimed that God had told her to drive out the English. By 1450 the French had driven the English out of Normandy. By 1453 the English had lost all their lands in France except the port of Calais.

THE HUNDRED YEARS WAR - THINK AGAIN!

There never was a war that lasted one hundred years. During the 'hundred years' there were times of fighting and times when there was no fighting at all.

More importantly, wars between England and France had been going on since the Norman Conquest . Henry I fought wars against the king of France as did Henry II, Richard I and John. The French king was meant to be the overlord of the French lands of the kings of England and there was often trouble between the rulers of France and England. King John lost all of his French lands except for Gascony in south-west France. The Hundred Years War was fought to protect this area and to extend English power in France.

NEW WORDS

INSANE: mentally ill and unable to think clearly and make plans.

Joan of Arc

Joan was born in 1412. At the age of 13 she claimed that saints were telling her to go to the French prince, Charles, and help him save France from the English.

Charles believed her and gave her knights and a white suit of armour. Joan went on to defeat the English at several battles and was beside Charles when he was crowned king of France in 1429.

*Joan was helped in her war with the English by the fact that the English, had a very young king instead of an experienced general as their ruler. Also, France was uniting against the way it was being treated by the English. Its new king was also a stronger ruler than his **insane** father had been.*

In 1430 she was captured by the Duke of Burgundy and handed over to his English friends. They said she was a witch and burnt her at the stake. The king of France made no attempt to save her. In 1920 she was made a saint.

So many French were killed at the sea battle of Sluys, in 1340, that the English joked that there was so much French blood in the sea, the fish could speak French.

WHY DID THE WAR LAST SUCH A LONG TIME?

If the English won so many battles, why did the war last so long? And why did the English lose it?

The English were never strong enough to completely defeat the French. Even if they had been, it was hard enough to run England without having to run France too. Also, the French disliked being ruled by English people. So, why did the Hundred Years War last so long?

- England was so rich it could pay for years of war.
- England had so much experience of war against the Welsh and Scots, it could use this against France.

- England had a well organised army of paid soldiers. The French had an old fashioned feudal army.
- English nobles supported the war, as they made money from lands and goods taken from the French.
- France was a powerful country but disunited. The English worked with the French king's enemies. But in 1435 the Duke of Burgundy changed sides. He then helped the French defeat the English.
- When Henry V attacked France, the French king was insane and could not organise a defence.

SOURCE A

▲ A fifteenth century French painting of English archers at the battle of Crecy, 1346. These paid soldiers of the English king slaughtered the advancing French nobles and knights with a storm of arrows.

Q 1. Make a timeline of the events of the Hundred Years War. Mark on it any 'turning points'. These are events which changed history. Explain why you chose these as 'turning points'.

2. 'The Hundred Years War was a war the English could never really win.' Explain why this was so.

- Describe problems faced by England in ruling France.
- Explain why the war went on for so long. Mention English strengths and French weaknesses.
- Explain why the English started to lose and how the war ended.

The Wars of the Roses

WHAT WERE THE WARS OF THE ROSES?

Between 1455 and 1485 two rival groups in the English royal family fought each other for the right to rule England. These battles became known later as 'The Wars of the Roses'. This was because the badge of one side – the Lancastrians – was a red rose and the badge of the other side – the Yorkists – was a white rose. They were both descended from two sons of Edward III.

The Wars of the Roses

1399 Richard II overthrown by his cousin the Duke of Lancaster, who became Henry IV.

Henry IV became King followed by Henry V and Henry VI.

1455 Richard, Duke of York, took control from Henry VI.

1460 Henry VI's wife, Margaret, killed Richard, Duke of York.

1461 Richard's son, Edward, Duke of York, captured Henry VI and made himself King Edward IV.

1470 Edward driven out of England. Henry VI put back on throne.

1471 Edward returns. Henry VI murdered. Edward king again.

1483 Edward died. His brother, Richard III, put Edward's two sons in prison and became king. Probably murdered the two princes.

1485 Henry Tudor killed Richard III at Battle of Bosworth. Became Henry VII.

THE DEATH OF RICHARD III AND THE START OF 'TUDOR ENGLAND'

In 1485, Henry Tudor (a Lancastrian) fought and killed Richard III (a Yorkist) at the Battle of Bosworth. Richard had been a popular leader when he first became king in 1483. He was an experienced soldier and a strong ruler who had fought hard for his elder brother, King Edward IV. Even when he locked up his dead brother's young sons in the Tower of London he remained popular. He seemed to promise strong rule and peace. But soon rumours were spreading that King Richard had murdered his young nephews and many of his supporters turned against him. Because of this, even though Henry Tudor did not have a very strong claim to the throne he found quite a few people supported him when he landed in Wales in August 1485. Two weeks later he killed Richard in a battle in which many of Richard's men betrayed him. A new family – the Tudors – had become rulers.. But would they last? Many people living at the time were not sure? Only time would tell...

SOURCE A

In a period of more than 30 years, the total time spent actually at war was about one year. Economic, social and religious life went on as before. The temporary problems which the wars caused to the aristocracy was real enough. But it made little difference to the way the country was run.

⚊ **Historical Atlas of Britain,** *1981*

SOURCE B

The crown of England had changed hands several times over the past thirty years. Now all the Yorkist leaders were dead except Edward, Earl of Warwick, and he was safely imprisoned in the Tower where he was murdered in 1499. The Wars of the Roses were at an end and the Tudor **dynasty** finally secure.

⚊ *Philip Haigh,* **The Military Campaigns of the Wars of the Roses,** *1995*

SOURCE C

The great families of the barons died in the turmoil they had started. They perished, however, alone. The Wars of the Roses hardly touched the common people. So except for some local problems the country did well enough; its industries continued to grow, its wool trade with Burgundy was not interupted; some older towns decayed, but new ones were springing up.

⚊ *G.Warner and C.Marten,* **The Groundwork of British History,** *1923.*

Q How did the Wars of the Roses affect life in England? Write a mini-essay to explain:

- What the wars were about and when and how they were fought.
- The impact on the noble families.
- The impact on ordinary people.
- How the wars ended and who won.
- How much they changed England.

Discussion Point
Is it ever right to use violence to oppose something you believe is unjust?

Win the Battle of Bosworth, 1485

YOUR MISSION: to help King Richard III win the Battle of Bosworth, on August 22, 1485.

A BATTLE BOUND TO BE LOST?

Richard III, the Yorkist king, was threatened by Henry Tudor, a Lancastrian. Henry landed in Wales and marched into England, wanting to kill King Richard. On August 22 the two armies faced each other near the village of Market Bosworth. But really there were three armies:

- Henry Tudor had an army of about 6,000 men.

- King Richard had an army of about 10,000 men. Richard was in charge of the middle part of the army. In the front the army was commanded by the Duke of Norfolk, a loyal friend of Richard's. Behind Richard the army was commanded by the Earl of Northumberland. This was an important part of the army – if Richard had problems these soldiers should help him. But Northumberland did not like him.

- The third army belonged to two brothers – Sir William Stanley and Thomas, Lord Stanley. They had been told to meet Richard at the battle and fight for him. But they did not like the king. When the battle started would they join in on his side, watch and do nothing, or join in on the side of Henry Tudor? No one knew. Together these two brothers had an army of 8,000 men.

The maps show you what happened in the battle. In the end the Stanley brothers joined Henry Tudor and King Richard was killed. But could he have won? Look at the evidence. Could you have helped him win?

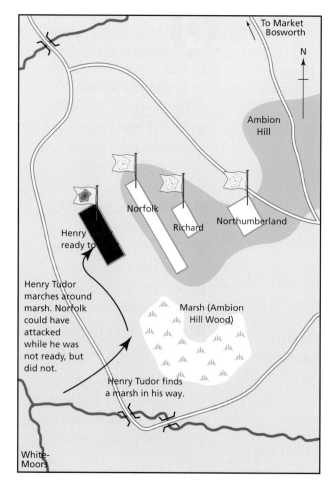

To Market Bosworth

N

Ambion Hill

Norfolk

Richard

Northumberland

Henry ready to

Henry Tudor marches around marsh. Norfolk could have attacked while he was not ready, but did not.

Marsh (Ambion Hill Wood)

Henry Tudor finds a marsh in his way.

White-Moors

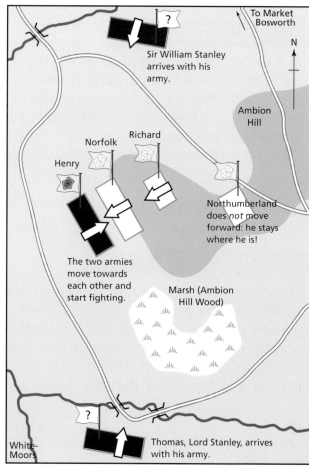

To Market Bosworth

N

Sir William Stanley arrives with his army.

Ambion Hill

Norfolk

Richard

Henry

Northumberland does *not* move forward: he stays where he is!

The two armies move towards each other and start fighting.

Marsh (Ambion Hill Wood)

White-Moors

Thomas, Lord Stanley, arrives with his army.

INVESTIGATION

You are a military advisor brought in to help King Richard III win the Battle of Bosworth.

1. First, explain how and why the battle was lost.

2. Now suggest different things Richard III could do which might help him win the battle. Below are some of the things he might do. Look at each one. Describe how it is different to what happened in 1485. Finally, decide which one of these you would advise him to choose and why it might help him win.

- Order Norfolk to attack the side of Henry Tudor's army, while it marched to one side of the marsh.
- Put Northumberland in the front of the army and make him be the first to attack Henry Tudor's army.
- Put Northumberland in the front of the army attacking Henry Tudor and take Norfolk and his men with you when you attack Henry Tudor as he rides towards Sir William Stanley.

Legend says that King Richard's gold crown was found under a thorn bush. Thomas, Lord Stanley put it on Henry's head and **proclaimed** him the new king. There is still a place called Crown Hill near the battlefield today.

NEW WORDS

PROCLAIMED: announce and tell people something important.

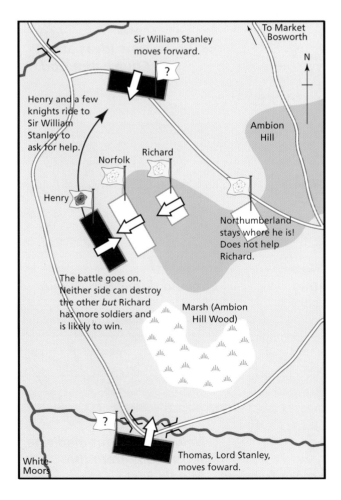

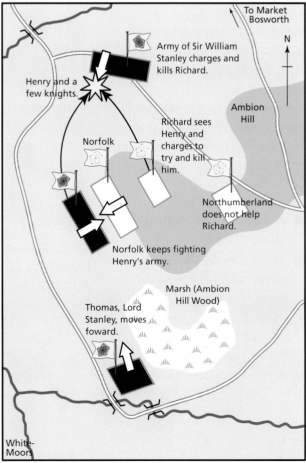

10 WHERE HAVE WE BEEN? WHERE DO WE GO FROM HERE?

THE END OF THE MIDDLE AGES?

Historians sometimes call the year 1485 the end of the Middle Ages, or Medieval period of history. This was when King Richard III was killed and Henry Tudor became King Henry VII. The Lancastrians had won the Wars of the Roses and a new family - the Tudors - had started to rule the country.

But this is just done to be tidy. There was really no great change in 1485. Most people living in Britain would have felt that life carried on much as it had done before. They did not know the Middle Ages had ended! Anyway, the name 'Middle Ages', or 'Medieval' was made up much later by historians. Absolutely no one used it at the time.

However, this is where this book ends. We have got to end somewhere and we have come a long way since 1066. Let's think about two main questions about 1485:

■ How had life changed since 1066?

■ How would life carry on after 1485 because of what had happened since 1066?

1485: WHAT HAS CHANGED SINCE 1066?

Changing royal families.
1066: Normans. 1154: Plantagenets.
1485: Tudors.

Population up and down.

Growth of towns.

New ideas about Church and God.

French lands lost.

England dominates Britain.

Invention of printing spreads ideas in books.

Parliament becoming powerful.

Peasants have more freedom.

New ideas about medicine, technology from the Middle East.

1485: WHERE DO WE GO FROM HERE?

The Tudors have enemies. Will they survive?

People are better-off. Will it continue?

> ## NEW WORDS
>
> **ENCLOSING:**
> surrounding land with hedges and controlling the right to use it. Keeping more sheep and growing less food for people.

Will parliament become even more powerful?

Christian Church is powerful – will it stay so?

Most exploration of the world done by Portugese and Spanish. Will England take a bigger part?

Population is rising. Will this mean more poor people?

Rich farmers are enclosing *land. Will even more land be enclosed for sheep?*

Q 1. From what you can see in this BIG PICTURE and from what you have seen in the rest of the book, imagine you are a peasant from 1066 who has been carried forward in time to 1485.

Explain how life has changed since your day.

Also explain anything that you think has stayed the same.

2. Copy the questions from 1485: WHERE DO WE GO FROM HERE? As you continue to study history, record the answers you discover to these questions.

Discussion Point
Would you prefer to live in Britain today, or during the Middle Ages?